Affirmative Counseling for Transgender and Gender Diverse Clients

About the Authors

lore m. dickey, PhD, ABPP, is a licensed and board-certified counseling psychologist. His work in the field of psychology has included serving as a faculty member at both the undergraduate and graduate levels. Most recently he was a behavioral health consultant at North Country HealthCare, a federally qualified health center in Flagstaff, AZ. Although lore is retired, he is actively engaged in writing and speaking about the lives of trans people.

Jae A. Puckett, PhD, is a licensed clinical psychologist. They are an assistant professor at Michigan State University where they also direct Trans-ilience: The Transgender Stress and Resilience Research Team as well as supervise graduate trainees in the Sexual and Gender Minority Clinic. Dr. Puckett has published numerous articles on the experiences of stress and resilience in the lives of transgender and gender diverse individuals and about affirming clinical practice, in addition to teaching, training, and supervising those providing clinical services to trans clients

Advances in Psychotherapy – Evidence-Based Practice

Series Editor
Danny Wedding, PhD, MPH, Professor Emeritus, University of Missouri–Saint Louis

Associate Editors
Jonathan S. Comer, PhD, Professor of Psychology and Psychiatry, Director of Mental Health Interventions and Technology (MINT) Program, Center for Children and Families, Florida International University, Miami, FL

J. Kim Penberthy, PhD, ABPP, Professor of Psychiatry & Neurobehavioral Sciences, University of Virginia, Charlottesville, VA

Kenneth E. Freedland, PhD, Professor of Psychiatry and Psychology, Washington University School of Medicine, St. Louis, MO

Linda C. Sobell, PhD, ABPP, Professor, Center for Psychological Studies, Nova Southeastern University, Ft. Lauderdale, FL

The basic objective of this series is to provide therapists with practical, evidence-based treatment guidance for the most common disorders seen in clinical practice – and to do so in a reader-friendly manner. Each book in the series is both a compact "how-to" reference on a particular disorder for use by professional clinicians in their daily work and an ideal educational resource for students as well as for practice-oriented continuing education.

The most important feature of the books is that they are practical and easy to use: All are structured similarly and all provide a compact and easy-to-follow guide to all aspects that are relevant in real-life practice. Tables, boxed clinical "pearls," marginal notes, and summary boxes assist orientation, while checklists provide tools for use in daily practice.

Continuing Education Credits

Psychologists and other healthcare providers may earn five continuing education credits for reading the books in the *Advances in Psychotherapy* series and taking a multiple-choice exam. This continuing education program is a partnership of Hogrefe Publishing and the National Register of Health Service Psychologists. Details are available at https://www.hogrefe.com/us/cenatreg

The National Register of Health Service Psychologists is approved by the American Psychological Association to sponsor continuing education for psychologists. The National Register maintains responsibility for this program and its content.

Advances in Psychotherapy – Evidence-Based Practice, Volume 45

Affirmative Counseling for Transgender and Gender Diverse Clients

lore m. dickey
Former Behavioral Health Consultant at North Country HealthCare, Flagstaff, AZ

Jae A. Puckett
Department of Psychology, Michigan State University, East Lansing, MI

Library of Congress of Congress Cataloging in Publication information for the print version of this book is available via the Library of Congress Marc Database under the Library of Congress Control Number 2022931436

Library and Archives Canada Cataloguing in Publication

Title: Affirmative counseling for transgender and gender diverse clients / lore m. dickey, former Behavioral Health Consultant at North Country HealthCare, Flagstaff, AZ, Jae A. Puckett, Department of Psychology, Michigan State University, East Lansing, MI.
Names: dickey, lore m., 1961- author. | Puckett, Jae A., author.
Series: Advances in psychotherapy--evidence-based practice ; v. 45.
Description: Series statement: Advances in psychotherapy--evidence-based practice ; volume 45 | Includes bibliographical references.
Identifiers: Canadiana (print) 20220165963 | Canadiana (ebook) 20220166048 | ISBN 9780889375130 (softcover) | ISBN 9781616765132 (PDF) | ISBN 9781613345139 (EPUB)
Subjects: LCSH: Transgender people—Counseling of. | LCSH: Gender-nonconforming people—Counseling of. | LCSH: Transgender people—Mental health services. | LCSH: Gender-nonconforming people—Mental health services.
Classification: LCC HQ77.9 .D53 2022 | DDC 155.3/3—dc23

© 2023 by Hogrefe Publishing

www.hogrefe.com

The authors and publisher have made every effort to ensure that the information contained in this text is in accord with the current state of scientific knowledge, recommendations, and practice at the time of publication. In spite of this diligence, errors cannot be completely excluded. Also, due to changing regulations and continuing research, information may become outdated at any point. The authors and publisher disclaim any responsibility for any consequences which may follow from the use of information presented in this book.

Registered trademarks are not noted specifically as such in this publication. The use of descriptive names, registered names, and trademarks does not imply, even in the absence of a specific statement, that such names are exempt from the relevant protective laws and regulations and therefore free for general use.

The cover image is an agency photo depicting models. Use of the photo on this publication does not imply any connection between the content of this publication and any person depicted in the cover image.
Cover image: © Bulat Silvia – iStock.com

PUBLISHING OFFICES

USA:	Hogrefe Publishing Corporation, 44 Merrimac St., Suite 207, Newburyport, MA 01950 Phone 978 255 3700; E-mail customerservice@hogrefe.com
EUROPE:	Hogrefe Publishing GmbH, Merkelstr. 3, 37085 Göttingen, Germany Phone +49 551 99950 0, Fax +49 551 99950 111; E-mail publishing@hogrefe.com

SALES & DISTRIBUTION

USA:	Hogrefe Publishing, Customer Services Department, 30 Amberwood Parkway, Ashland, OH 44805 Phone 800 228 3749, Fax 419 281 6883; E-mail customerservice@hogrefe.com
UK:	Hogrefe Publishing, c/o Marston Book Services Ltd., 160 Eastern Ave., Milton Park, Abingdon, OX14 4SB Phone +44 1235 465577, Fax +44 1235 465556; E-mail direct.orders@marston.co.uk
EUROPE:	Hogrefe Publishing, Merkelstr. 3, 37085 Göttingen, Germany Phone +49 551 99950 0, Fax +49 551 99950 111; E-mail publishing@hogrefe.com

OTHER OFFICES

CANADA:	Hogrefe Publishing Corporation, 82 Laird Drive, East York, Ontario M4G 3V1
SWITZERLAND:	Hogrefe Publishing, Länggass-Strasse 76, 3012 Bern

No part of this book may be reproduced, stored in a retrieval system or transmitted, in any form or by any means, electronic, mechanical, photocopying, microfilming, recording or otherwise, without written permission from the publisher.

Printed and bound in the USA

ISBN 978-0-88937-513-0 (print) • ISBN 978-1-61676-513-2 (PDF) • ISBN 978-1-61334-513-9 (EPUB)
https://doi.org/10.1027/00513-000

Contents

1	**Description**	1
1.1	Terminology	1
1.2	Definitions	2
1.3	Overview	8
1.3.1	Indigenous People	8
1.3.2	Medical Model	8
1.3.3	Transgender Movement	11
1.3.4	Nonbinary Movement	11
1.3.5	Overview of Affirming Practice	12
1.4	Gatekeeping	13
2	**Theories and Models**	16
2.1	Minority Stress Theory	17
2.1.1	Tailoring Minority Stress Theory to Trans People	18
2.1.2	Suicide and Minority Stress	21
2.2	Gender Dysphoria	21
2.2.1	Reclassifying Gender Dysphoria	23
2.3	Medical Necessity	23
2.4	Informed Consent	25
2.5	Harm Reduction	25
2.6	Shaping the Therapeutic Dialogue	26
2.6.1	Introducing Yourself With Your Pronoun(s)	26
2.6.2	Presentation of Experience and Training	28
2.6.3	Avoid Assumptions About What an Identity Term Means for the Client	29
2.6.4	Trans Client Fluidity in Their Gender and Sexuality	29
2.6.5	Avoid Assumptions About Transition	30
2.6.6	How to Respond When You Make a Mistake	30
2.6.7	Understanding Diverse Experiences of Gender	31
2.6.8	Review the Client Experience in Your Practice	31
2.6.9	Knowledge of Local Resources	32
2.7	Nuanced Clinical Topics	33
2.7.1	Grief	33
2.7.2	Suicide and Trans People	34
2.7.3	Nonsuicidal Self-Injury	35
2.7.4	Reasonably Well-Controlled Mental Health	35
2.7.5	Regret	37
3	**Assessment and Treatment Indications**	39
3.1	Assessment	39
3.1.1	Screening Tools	39
3.1.2	Outcome Measures	40
3.1.3	Critique of Personality Assessment Tools	41
3.1.4	Progress-Monitoring Tools	42

| 3.1.5 | Measures Designed for Trans Clients | 42 |
| 3.1.6 | Caution When Interpreting Results | 45 |

4 Treatment — 46
4.1	Method of Treatment	46
4.1.1	Specific Clinical Concerns	46
4.2	Efficacy and Prognosis	49
4.2.1	Affirmative Practice	50
4.2.2	Therapeutic Approaches	52
4.3	Variations of the Method: Letter Writing	58
4.4	Problems in Carrying Out Treatments	61
4.4.1	Trauma	62
4.4.2	Trans Clients in Rural Locations	63
4.4.3	Autism Spectrum Disorder in Trans People	64
4.4.4	Co-Occurring Medical Concerns	66
4.4.5	Persistence, Insistence, and Consistence	68
4.5	Multicultural Issues	68
4.5.1	Intersectionality	69
4.6	Importance of Interrogating Your Gender	71
4.7	Problematic Treatments	72
4.7.1	Conversion Therapy	72
4.7.2	Rapid Onset Gender Dysphoria	74

5 Case Vignettes — 76

6 Further Reading — 83

7 References — 84

8 Appendix: Tools and Resources — 93

1

Description

Although transgender and nonbinary individuals are in the minority, being trans is not so uncommon as to be invisible. Trans people have existed throughout history, and being trans is not a new phenomenon. It has been estimated that there are 1.4 million trans people in the US (Flores et al., 2016). Flores and colleagues suggest that the number of trans people in the US could be as high as 2.3 million and as low as 845,000, given statistically credible intervals.

This means that there are as many trans people in the US as there are inhabitants of some cities such as Indianapolis (population 864,447 in 2019), Honolulu (population 348,985 in 2019), Phoenix (population 1.6 million in 2019), Philadelphia (population 1.6 million in 2019), or Houston (population 2.3 million in 2019). Trans people are a subpopulation in the US, and they are often disregarded or turned away from services and care.

In the field of psychology, discussions of the needs of trans people have often been addressed in courses such as abnormal psychology, behavioral pathology, or human sexuality. In each of these course offerings, trans people are typically conceptualized from a deficit perspective, and many of the textbooks used have inaccurate or offensive descriptions of the experiences of trans people. This means that those who are trained to work in clinical settings may only learn about the diagnostic nomenclature found in the *Diagnostic and Statistical Manual of Mental Disorders,* fifth edition (DSM-5; American Psychiatric Association, 2013). There are times when it is appropriate to view trans people's experiences through the lens of the DSM. This might include referrals for medical care, where the provider or the insurance company requires a diagnosis. But medical care is *not* a goal for some trans people, and there are many other reasons a trans person might seek mental health care. If a provider is only viewing their work with a trans person from a medicalized approach, they are at best likely to miss important clinical concerns, and at worst, to alienate and pathologize them.

There may be as many as 2.3 million trans people in the United States (ca. 0.95% of the population)

Deficit models and conceptualizations are harmful to trans people

1.1 Terminology

Transgender, nonbinary, and gender diverse people may use a variety of terms to describe their gender identity. In this volume, we will use the term "trans" as we describe the ways to work with these communities. We acknowledge that the term "trans" may not fit for some people under these broader umbrellas; however, it is the most inclusive term being used as this volume is being written.

"Trans" is used by some people whose gender identity differs from what was assigned at birth

We describe the lives of trans people below using terms that are commonly used. The list of terms below, in Section 1.2: Definitions, is far from being exhaustive, and psychologists are encouraged to be mindful of the need to talk with their clients about the terms that best describe their identity. Trans people may use terms that shift over time. The ability to be flexible with your clients is vital. Inflexibility is likely to lead to a fracture in the clinical relationship. The result could be catastrophic for your trans clients.

Affirmative language is critical when addressing trans clients

The terms listed below (Section 1.2: Definitions) are relatively common in trans communities. It should be noted that there are many others that are less commonly used. These include "birl," "pangender," "hybrid," and "aggressive" (Harrison et al., 2012). Harrison and colleagues (2012) noted that over 850 different terms were used in the study they were reporting from. Given that the terms for which definitions are provided below are limited to some of the more commonly used, providers will benefit their clients by taking on the responsibility to learn about terms or identities that clients hold, outside of those listed below, as they come up in their clinical practices. Although it is helpful to learn the basic terms provided here, providers will need to seek out new education as they work with trans clients to broaden their knowledge and to continue to grow this awareness as terminology continues to evolve and change over time.

Some trans people eschew labels, others have self-affirmed terms used to describe their gender

1.2   Definitions

For readers' convenience, the terms are listed in alphabetical order.

Agender is a term used to by people who do not identify with a gender, those who identify as having a neutral gender, those who choose not to label their gender, those who feel detached from their gender, and those with other types of experiences in which a person does not identify with a specific gender. Like other categories, agender individuals may or may not seek medical means to affirm their gender. Making a medical transition is an individual decision, regardless of identity.

Some people do not identify with any gender

Bigender relates to people who feel as though two genders (not necessarily male and female or as a man or woman) are consistent with their felt identity. This is different from having an identity as third gender.

Bottom surgery includes the various genital surgeries. For a person assigned male at birth (AMAB), this includes an orchiectomy and a vaginoplasty. For a person assigned female at birth (AFAB), it includes a hysterectomy with or without oophorectomy, metoidioplasty, or phalloplasty (with or without a urethral extension), and a scrotoplasty. For many people, the cost of these procedures prohibits their ability to access care.

Surgeries can be prohibitively expensive for many trans people

Cisgender is a label that applies to any person whose gender is consistent or congruent with the sex they were assigned at birth. Another way of thinking about cisgender is that a cisgender person does not have a trans identity. Rather than referring to people in this group as not being transgender, it is important to specifically use the term "cisgender." Individuals who are in the dominant and majority group often have their identity treated as the norm and as such are not called on to have labels for their identities. Using the term "cisgender"

Cisgender people make up the majority of those in society – they have their own experience of gender helps to disrupt these power hierarchies and the ways that the cisgender experience is normalized. Not using the term cisgender can result in trans people being "othered" and marginalized.

Cisnormative refers to the assumption that a person's gender or gender identity is congruent, or consistent, with the sex they were assigned at birth. Assumptions regarding a person's gender can lead to inaccurate conclusions that can be harmful. This is similar to *cissexism* which involves the systemic marginalization of trans people, such as via discrimination based on their gender identity or gender expression.

Gender affirmative is the supportive approach to treatment that preferences and foregrounds the stories and lives of trans people. Gender-affirmative counseling has been defined as

> counseling that is culturally relevant and responsive to [trans] clients and their multiple social identities, addresses the influence of social inequities on the lives of [trans] clients, enhances [trans] client resilience and coping, advocates to reduce systemic barriers to [trans] mental and physical health, and leverages [trans] client's strengths. (Singh & dickey, 2017, p. 4)

Gender binary is a construct that assumes that there are two, and only two, immutable gender expressions and gender identities that align with these (masculine and feminine expressions that align with identifying as a man or a woman, respectively).

Gender creative is a term that is typically used with children (rather than adults). Children with a gender creative identity may still be in an exploration phase.

Gender diverse can be used to describe people whose gender identity differs from the sex they were assigned at birth. This is considered by some to be a more inclusive and nonpathological term that is intended to be inclusive of all trans people. Some in the trans community do not like using this term to refer to trans people, as they believe that all people, cisgender or trans, have diversity in the ways they understand their gender. This term tends to be used within academic circles rather than in the trans community.

Gender dysphoria is a medical or diagnostic term that is used in the DSM-5 (American Psychiatric Association, 2013). Not all trans people will endorse symptoms consistent with the diagnostic criteria. This is due, in part, to the ways that gender dysphoria is embedded in medicine – which may not fit for the client(s) you are working with. Broadly speaking, gender dysphoria refers to distress arising due to discordance between one's current gender experience and their body, gender expression, or gender identity that was assigned at birth.

Gender expansive is a term that has been used to describe children who do not identify their gender with the sex they were assigned at birth. This term is less pathological than others that have been used.

Genderflux refers to an experience of gender in which the intensity of the person's gender identity changes over time. In some moments a person may strongly experience their gender in a particular way whereas at other times this may not be as strong.

Medical terms such as "gender dysphoria" and "gender incongruence" should not be used as identity labels

Children may use terms that are more welcoming and affirming such as "gender creative" or "expansive"

Gender identity refers to the way in which a person experiences their gender. Gender is a social construct that includes rules or expectations for how a person will behave that are imposed on people based on the sex they were assigned at birth or another's perception of their gender. Everyone has a gender and a gender identity. Cisgender people rarely think about what it means to have a gender, just as heterosexual people rarely think about their sexual orientation.

Gender identity change efforts (GICEs) are problematic and unethical clinical approaches to working with trans people (usually children) in an effort to change their gender identity to be consistent with the sex they were assigned at birth. Also known as *conversion therapy*, it is a harmful approach and is outlawed in many US states.

Gender incongruence is the diagnostic label used by the World Health Organization (WHO) in the *International Classification of Diseases*, 11th edition (ICD-11; see WHO, n.d.) to describe gender dysphoria.

Genderqueer is a term that has been used for many years by people who have identities that do not fall into designations of women and men and are deliberate about the ways they play with gender. For some people, this may mean that their gender is outside of binary understandings of gender or somewhere along a spectrum of gender experiences. The individual experience of genderqueer people in terms of how a person describes their gender varies across persons, and there is no one way to be genderqueer. For some genderqueer people, this identity label is also a form of a political statement. Some people within this category may align with a nonbinary identity or a trans identity. Just like any other trans and gender diverse person, they may or may not seek to affirm their gender through medical means.

> Understanding what the term genderqueer means for each individual client is important

Harm reduction is an approach to care that comes from substance abuse treatment. When applied to trans health, a provider who is working with a client who is accessing hormones from the Internet or friends will continue to receive medically supervised hormone treatment. Some providers may feel that it is necessary to stop a person's hormone treatment if the use of hormones is not medically supervised. In using a harm reduction approach, the client is able to continue the use of hormones as they engage with a provider. This allows the client to avoid unnecessary disruption of hormone treatment.

> A client without access to a safe supply of hormones should not be required to stop treatment

Hormone therapy is a medical treatment in which some trans people engage. A person who was AFAB will be prescribed testosterone. A person who was AMAB will take an androgen blocker and a feminizing hormone (usually estradiol). Some people refer to this as "hormone replacement therapy," which is a term used for cisgender people, especially women who are in, or have passed, menopause. In trans people, we are not "replacing" hormones, rather, we are introducing cross-sex hormones.

> Hormone therapy is no longer a one-size fits all treatment

Informed consent is a process whereby trans people have the opportunity to demonstrate their understanding of hormone treatment or a surgical procedure without the addition of more elaborate evaluation procedures or other barriers to care. This knowledge allows the provider to ascertain the need for additional support or education of a trans person to ensure they are prepared for the medical procedure they are seeking. In using an informed consent model of treatment, trans people are able to access care without having to experience undue and unnecessary barriers.

> Using an informed consent model of treatment can facilitate access to care

Neutrois is a term used by some people to identify their gender as being neutral. This is not exactly the same as agender. As stated for other identities, a person who identifies as neutrois may desire to make changes to their body to align with a more congruent sense of self.

Nonbinary or gender nonbinary is used by trans people who eschew the gender binary. There are many ways that nonbinary people may experience their gender, such as viewing gender as fluid, existing along a spectrum, or experiencing their gender at multiple places along this spectrum simultaneously. Similar to other trans people, a person with a nonbinary identity may or may not engage in a medical transition (see Section 1.3.2: Medical Model). Nonbinary people may also use alternative pronouns to the ones associated with the gender binary. Instead of "she/her" or "he/him" as pronouns, a nonbinary person may use "they/them/their," "zi," "hir," or other pronouns (see Section 2.6.1: Introducing Yourself With Your Pronoun(s)). Additionally, not all nonbinary people identify with the term "transgender" or "trans," and the term "nonbinary" can be viewed as another umbrella term encompassing other identities like genderqueer and genderfluid. Even so, each individual client will have their own experience of their gender or identity terms that best fit with them and which may fall outside of common descriptions (e.g., some genderqueer people may not identify with the term "nonbinary").

> Gender is fluid and exists on a spectrum – not two immutable poles

> There is a plethora of terms used within the trans community

Standards of Care (SOC) for the Health of Transsexual, Transgender, and Gender Nonconforming People are published by the World Professional Association for Transgender Health (WPATH; https://www.wpath.org). As of this writing, the current version (ver. 7) was released in 2011 (WPATH, 2012). The 8th version of the SOC is in development and is expected to be released in 2022. It will be critical for psychologists to work from the most recent version of the SOC. Choosing not to use the most updated version of the SOC (or any other set of guidelines or recommendations) may be considered unethical behavior and cause harm to the client.

> Some medical providers or insurance companies will adhere to the SOC

Third gender is a term used by some people who do not identify their gender as being consistent with the sex they were assigned at birth. This term may be used by some Native American people, as it recognizes that there are more than two genders. The notion of there only being two binary genders is often viewed as a product of colonization.

> Many terms are used by Native American people – psychologists should always mirror the terms used by their clients

Top surgery for a person AFAB includes chest masculinization (e.g., double incision or keyhole top surgery techniques). For people AMAB it can include breast augmentation and other surgical procedures that are targeted at feminizing a person. There are other forms of surgical care that trans feminine individuals may seek out, such as facial feminization surgery (also known as FFS).

> For trans clients seeking surgery, it is important to remember that this is medically necessary care

Trans man or trans woman are common terms used to describe a person based on their *lived* gender identity. A person who is AFAB and identifies their current gender identity as a man may identify themselves as a trans man. The opposite is true for someone who was AMAB and identifies their current gender as a woman (trans woman). It is important to note that trans people may not identify with the term "trans." Rather, they may identify as a man or a woman. It is not necessary for trans men and trans women to obtain any gender-affirming medical care to align with these identities, although that certainly may be part of an individual's processes for affirming their gender. You may also sometimes see these terms written as

> AFAB and AMAB have replaced outdated terms such as natal or biological sex

"transman," "transwoman," "male-to-female" (MTF), or "female-to-male" (FTM). However, these terms tend to be less widely used and may be offensive for some trans people. For some trans people, discomfort with FTM and MTF may be related to the fact that these assume binary starting and ending points and perpetually note a person's sex assigned at birth. Although the terms AMAB and AFAB also assume a starting point, this is less problematic for trans people than FTM and MTF.

> **Transgender people are not defined by the presence or absence of genitals**

Transgender is both an individual and a collective term. The term was coined by Virginia Prince in the early 1990s (Ekins & King, 2005). Prince reportedly did not want to be defined by her genitals and felt that she could be a woman without the need for genital surgery. Some trans people choose not to take hormones or have surgery (Puckett et al., 2018). Others may use a combination of hormones and surgery that fit for their experience of gender. Other trans people may desire medical care to affirm their gender but lack access due to insurance issues or lack of finances. Collectively, transgender is used as an umbrella term and is thought to be inclusive of all people who have a gender identity that is different from the sex they were assigned at birth.

Transition is the process whereby an individual takes steps to bring their gender in line with their felt sense of who they are as a gendered person. A person may complete a social transition, which can include using a different name and pronouns, changing the manner in which they dress, and changing their hairstyle. For children, a social transition may be the only available option. A legal transition can involve making changes to identification documents (e.g., driver's license, birth certificate, and passport) through the courts or other administrative processes. Legal transitions can also include changing your name and gender marker. These processes vary based on the jurisdiction where a person lives or was born. The National Center for Transgender Equality has a number of resources that will help a person understand the rules and laws where they live or were born (https://transequality.org/documents).

> **There are three types of transition: social, medical, and legal**

Finally, a trans person might make a medical transition. A medical transition can include a combination of hormone treatment and surgical interventions. The need for referral to a physician for hormones or surgery will be different from one client to the next. It is important to keep in mind that each trans person you see may have different goals for a medical transition. Making the assumption that a trans person wants hormones or surgery is a dangerous assumption, as there are many ways a person can make a transition. Medical interventions are not accessed by all trans people. Reasons for this might include a lack of desire for medical treatment, an inability to pay for care, a lack of providers, or medical or mental health contraindications. It is becoming increasingly common for "transition" to be referred to as "affirmation" instead.

> **A less common term is transsexual**

Transsexual is a term that is deeply rooted in the medical model (see Section 1.3.2: Medical Model) of transition. This term arose out of the work of Magnus Hirschfeld and David O. Cauldwell (dickey, 2020). Cauldwell first used the term to provide common language for people who engaged in a medical transition. Hirschfeld popularized the term over time. "Transsexual" is used much less often in the present day, and psychologists are cautioned against using this term unless a client asks that it be used to identify themselves.

A variation of the term "transsexual" is **true transsexual**. "True transsexual" was first used by Harry Benjamin (1966) to categorize transsexual people. Benjamin classified transsexual people into three groups and within those groups there were types. Types V and VI were moderate and high intensity "true transsexuals" (Benjamin, 1966). Trans people who were able to avail themselves of all medical interventions began to use the term "true transsexual" for themselves. Most often this was by trans women. In recent years, the term has taken on a derogatory tone. People who identify as true transsexuals feel that they are superior to trans people who do not or cannot make a full medical transition. The first author of this present volume was told by a transsexual woman that he could not self-identify as a transsexual, about 1 year after he started his transition. He was told, in no uncertain terms, that unless he had genital surgery, he would be a transgender person and could not identify as a transsexual. Being able to make a full medical transition is indicative of the ability to find providers who can carry out the care, having the resources to take time away from work for postsurgical healing, and being able to afford care.

> Some trans people do not want or cannot afford a medical transition

The idea that a person is a true transsexual led to people being told, or having it implied, that "they are not trans enough." This invalidation of trans people has the effect of marginalizing many within the community. Trans people have enough challenges in life that they do not need this type of mistreatment from within the trans community. Unfortunately, trans people are often told that they are not trans enough, including by medical and mental health providers, and this is never a well-meaning sentiment. As described here, this restrictive understanding of trans people from the medical profession may be internalized even within community members. If you are working with a trans person who has been told they are not trans enough or has come to believe that sentiment about themselves – regardless of the source – it will be important to process this and work through the ways that this informs the client's identity. There are many ways that a trans person might identify, present themselves, and relate to others. None of these are the "wrong" way to be trans. Each trans person should be able to make their own way in the world and not feel as though others are policing their identity.

> The idea that a person is "trans enough" is fraught with problems

Two-spirit is a term that is used in some Native American tribal communities. Two-spirit may indicate a person has a lesbian, gay, or bisexual (LGB) identity or that they have a trans identity.

There are a number of terms that have been used in the past that are no longer appropriate to use. Included are the terms "tranny," "natal sex," "transgendered," "sex reassignment" or "sex change," and "biological sex." Your clients may use terminology that is not listed here. Using the terminology used by a client is important, as it reflects an understanding and respect for the client. This is especially important when clients talk about their genitals. A trans person may not use medically correct terms when referring to parts of their body. As a provider, we can and should match our client's language and understand what the issues are regarding other terms that may not be affirming for the individual.

1.3 Overview

Trans, nonbinary, and gender diverse people have existed throughout history (dickey, 2020). Trans people were also present in indigenous cultures. Table 1 shows a list of many of the names which are or have been used to identify trans people throughout the world. This list is an example of the many people who have been embraced by their indigenous culture and may have been decimated as the result of colonization (dickey, 2020). In recent years, there has been a resurgence of trans people across the world. Although the acceptance of trans people is mixed from one country or jurisdiction to another, we continue to see trans people in day-to-day life and have a growing awareness of their life experiences.

Trans people have existed throughout history

1.3.1 Indigenous People

The idea that there are only two genders has led to the pathologization, and in some cultures, the decimation of people who lived in a third or fourth gender space. Colonization is largely responsible for this occurrence. Singh (2016) discusses the ways that *hijras* (the term used for people with a nonbinary gender identity in India and Pakistan) thrived prior to British colonization. Even today, the hijra continue to experience health disparities and they no longer hold the place of reverence they once had in their culture (Singh, 2016).

Colonization has resulted in belief systems and ways of living being forced upon others

Native American people who live in what is now known as North America have had similar experiences. In this case, it was typically the efforts of Christian settlers and missionaries that sought to colonize tribal communities. The expectation from the settlers was that members of the tribal community would have either a female or male identity. Like hijras (and other indigenous trans people), people who are now known in some tribes as two-spirit often held a place of reverence within their community. Not only were these tribal leaders forced to live in a way that was inconsistent with their felt sense of gender, but they also lost their place of respect. Just like trans labels that are no longer used, there are terms that were previously used for Native Americans (e.g., "berdache" and "winkte") that should no longer be used. One of the reasons for ceasing use of these terms is that they may have a very negative connotation and were not selected by Native Americans, rather white people chose the terms (an extensive list of terms used for trans people around the world can be found in Table 1).

Terminology that was created by someone other than who it is used to describe is often inappropriate

1.3.2 Medical Model

In the 1960s, there was a shift in the acceptance of the medical needs of trans people. Although medical interventions including surgery had been used before, the work of Harry Benjamin, MD (Benjamin, 1966; dickey, 2020), made this care more accessible during this specific period. Benjamin, a leader in trans health care for his time, was one of the first people to suggest that hormone treatment and surgery were medically necessary. The medical necessity was related to the ways that hormones and surgery would alleviate the distress

Harry Benjamin was one of the first to recognize the concept and the application of medical necessity

Table 1
Worldwide terms for trans people

Trans people	Culture
Acaults	Myanmar
Akava'ine	Cook Islands
Alyha, Hwame	Mohave tribe
Ankole[a]	Uganda
Ashtime[b]	Maale, Ethiopia
Bakla, Tom	Philippines
Bangala[a]	Democratic Republic of Congo
Biza'ah, Muxe	Mexico
Burrneesha	Albania
Calabai/Calalai/Bissu	Sulawesi, Indonesia
Chuckchi	Siberia
Dilbaa, Nádleehí	Navajo tribe
Fa'afafine	Samoa
Fakaleiti	Tonga
Femminiello[a]	Italy
Guevedoche	Dominican Republic
Hijra, Khawaja sira[b], Khusra[b], Zenana/Zenani	India and Pakistan
Katohey, Tom	Thailand
Köçek[a]	Ottoman Empire
Kothi, Sak veng/Srey sros	West Bengal and India
Kteuy	Cambodia
Lhamana	Zuni tribe
Mahu	Hawai'i and Polynesia
Mak Nyah	Malaysia
Mamluk[a]	Egypt
Mashoga	Kenya and Tanzania
Metis	Nepal
Mino	Benin
Mukhannthun[a]	Early Islamic Arabia

Table 1. Continued

Trans people	Culture
Narnban[b]	Pakistan
Ninauposkitzipxpe	Blackfoot tribe
Quariwarmi[a]	Inca, Peru
Sekrata	Madagascar
Sistergirl/Brotherboy	Australia
Skoptsy[a]	Russia
Third gender	South Asia
Tida wena	Venezuela
Tom, Waria	Indonesia
Travesti	Brazil
Two-Spirit	Native Americans
Wakatane, Whakawahine	Maori in New Zealand
Winkte	Lakota tribe
Xanith	Oman
X-jenda	Japan

Note. [a]Term is either no longer used, or people with this identity were directly impacted by colonization. [b]Typically translated as "eunuch."

a person was experiencing as a result of their gender not matching the sex they were assigned at birth.

Even though these changes in health care were being used more commonly, there were problems with the expectations imposed on trans people. One of the expectations was that a trans person would have a heterosexual sexual identity after the completion of transition. There was also the expectation that a trans person would want to complete all of the medical options that were available (e.g., hormones and surgery). Prior to beginning hormone treatment, a trans person was expected to engage in psychotherapy and complete a "real-life test or experience." This latter expectation was quite onerous for trans people. In some cases, living in one's self-affirmed gender without the benefit of surgery or hormones can place the individual at great risk for discrimination or violence.

> It was only when trans people themselves were on the revision team that the SOC requirements were relaxed

In 1979, the Harry Benjamin International Gender Dysphoria Association (now known as the World Professional Association for Transgender Health, or WPATH) published the first version of the SOC (Berger et al., 1979). Many of the expectations previously addressed were codified as result of its publication. Providers became curious as they heard similar stories from their clients about their gender history and the ways this impacted their life. Trans people quickly learned what they needed to tell a provider in order to gain access to care. The expectation of a singular narrative about one's gender history continued throughout the 1990s, emphasizing having known since a very early age that one was trans and wishing to complete all medical procedures. Although many providers now know that gender experiences and history vary from person to person, this history lingers and still influences care for some trans people.

1.3.3 Transgender Movement

Virginia Prince is credited with coining the term "transgender" (Ekins & King, 2005). Prince made it clear that her gender was her business, and the presence of genitals was not indicative of a person's felt gender. In time, the term "transgender" came to be used as a community term. As such, it is representative of anyone whose gender identity is different than the sex they were assigned at birth.

> **No one should be defined by the presence or absence of genitals**

Initially, though, as individuals began claiming a transgender identity, there was a split in the community, as those who were described as transsexual (meaning they had undergone medical gender affirmation) believed their gender experience to have more validity. This split was also influenced by the internalization of stigma from dominant discourse about trans people's lives. This is when the term "true transsexual" (first used by medical professionals; Benjamin, 1966) became especially problematic. People who believed themselves to be "true transsexuals" felt that their identity was more relevant because it assumed that a person had engaged in all of the available medical treatments (e.g., hormones and surgeries). It is not very common today for a trans person to use the identity label of "transsexual." This is not because people do not complete medical gender affirmation but rather because other identity labels have become more common (e.g., "trans woman" and "trans man"), and the term "transsexual" is deeply connected with the medical field and considered to indicate inherent pathology. The terms "female-to-male" and "male-to-female" have also fallen out of favor in the trans community. One of the reasons for this is that the terms FTM and MTF assume that there is a gender binary and not a gender spectrum. FTM and MTF leave no room for people with a nonbinary identity, and they perpetually connect a person to their sex assigned at birth, which may not be affirming for trans people.

> **There are many ways that the gender binary is reified in language today**

1.3.4 Nonbinary Movement

Although people with nonbinary identities have existed throughout history, there has been an increase in the numbers of people who have a nonbinary identity (Chang et al., 2018). People with nonbinary identities are likely to use pronouns that differ from those associated with the gender binary, although not always. This includes they/them/their, ey/em/eir, per, and other pronouns. This can be a challenge for people, especially cisgender individuals, who have had limited interaction with trans people, including those with nonbinary identities.

> **Pronouns can be and usually are very important for trans people, and these may change over time**

Nonbinary and gender diverse people face challenges in accessing gender-affirming care due to the binary narratives expected by some medical and mental health providers. Although all trans people may experience marginalization within mental health services, there are additional microaggressions that arise for nonbinary and gender diverse clients in the form of invalidating these gender identities, such as refusing to use gender neutral pronouns. Other ways people with nonbinary identities are discounted in the clinical setting begins with the paperwork clients are required to complete prior to or while accessing care. The demographic data required by clients typically includes sex (or gender) and marital status. The options that are provided tend to be cisnormative and heteronormative. This may leave trans people wondering if they are entering a clinical relationship that will be respectful of their identity.

> **Microaggressions, such as refusing to use correct pronouns, are harmful for people with nonbinary identities**

1.3.5 Overview of Affirming Practice

If a provider wants to indicate that they are trans inclusive, trans informed, or trans welcoming, they must communicate that in the most basic of ways. This includes not making assumptions about a trans person's identity; providing space for a trans client to self-identify using terms that fit for the client; and providing care in a space that is welcoming, affirming, and safe. Simple things, such as the kind of magazines that are available in the waiting room or the availability of all-gender restrooms, can make a big difference as to whether a trans person feels safe in a clinical space.

> **Trans people are often subjected to violence when using a restroom**

On this point, we are talking about ways that providers can create an environment of inclusion. Beyond the physical environment are the many ways that a provider interacts with a trans person that will indicate their affirmation of trans individuals. Interactions include the messages that can be found on a provider's website or social media platforms. Regularly using your pronouns in correspondence can send a subtle message to trans clients about your knowledge of trans communities.

Probably the most important thing for psychologists to remember is that each trans person has identity labels they use which are meaningful for them. When working with a trans person, it is important to make time to understand the terms that your clients use. Further, you may have two clients who use the same identity terms. This does not mean that each person defines those labels in the same way as each other or in the same way you have come to understand the term.

> **Some trans people avoid labels altogether as they find them to be offensive**

> **When you use the wrong pronoun(s), apologize and work harder to not make the mistake again**

You *will* make mistakes when referring to your trans clients. These mistakes are inevitable. It is critical that you own the mistake(s) and that your apology be brief. When psychologists take up extended amounts of time and space apologizing for their errors, it is often to ease their own discomfort rather than to remedy the mistake. Lengthy apologies also take away from the therapy hour and the time a client is paying for to receive support for their mental health needs.

In addition, you must learn from your mistakes. Providers need to do the work (e.g., interrogating your gender; see Section 4.6: Importance of Interrogating Your Gender) to ensure these mistakes do not happen repeatedly.

Such efforts should not be the emotional burden of trans clients – providers must take the initiative to address their own biases outside of the therapy room. For trainees, being able to address this in supervision will be important. For providers who are independently licensed, finding a consultation group will be helpful, as it provides a space for working through clinical challenges that are interfering with meeting the client's needs.

This book is intended to provide readers with up-to-date information about trans, nonbinary, and gender diverse people. The authors recognize that language can change within the trans communities and hope that readers will be sensitive to this as they work with clients. As would be the case for any person with a marginalized identity, making time to explore identity labels is critical. In fact, failing to take this step can have deleterious effects on the clinical relationship.

> Mirroring the language of the client will help to develop trust in the clinical relationship

Trans people have been and continue to be skeptical of the need to work with mental health providers. This is due to a long history of being forced into a gatekeeping relationship with mental health providers. Taking steps to be affirming and demonstrate this in overt and observable ways will help to build rapport and strong alliances with trans clients.

1.4 Gatekeeping

Gatekeeping is the process whereby mental health providers create unnecessary expectations that a client must conform to if they want support in moving forward with their transition. Examples of these expectations include, but are not limited to (a) a required number of counseling sessions (none are necessary), (b) the need to complete a "real-life test or experience," and (c) that the client does not have a diagnosable mental health condition or active symptoms of a mental health disorder (e.g., depression, anxiety, bipolar disorder, or post-traumatic stress disorder [PTSD]).

> Gatekeeping is problematic as it does not serve the needs of trans clients

The WPATH Standards of Care (WPATH, 2012) required some of these tasks in the past. However, there is no specific requirement for therapy, and trans people do not need to complete a real-life test or experience. Expecting these activities places an undue financial and social burden on the client. Further, although a trans person may meet the criteria for one or more mental health concerns (e.g., depression, anxiety, PTSD), this should not inherently disqualify a trans person from receiving gender-affirming care, without gaining a better understanding of the severity of the condition.

> Existing mental health problems should not automatically disqualify access to medical care

Even though the SOC since the 5th version, which was published in 1998, have stated that counseling, or psychotherapy, are not an absolute requirement for undergoing transition, there are providers who are still working under the assumption that counseling needs to happen (Levine et al., 1998). The first author of this present work recently saw a new patient who had been told by a medical provider that they needed 12 months of counseling before the initiation of hormone therapy. After working with the patient to help them understand how the first author approaches clinical work, it was important to then speak with the provider to ensure that they corrected their expectations regarding counseling requirements.

> There is no minimum number of counseling sessions a trans person must complete to access medical care

It should not be surprising that trans people are often skeptical of the motives of providers who are operating from archaic approaches to treatment. Information about such providers can quickly spread to trans people, and the provider may find that they see a reduction in the number of trans clients they are serving. The authors of this present work are very clear with trans and nonbinary clients in the initial session, about when counseling is or is not needed. Further, they make the conditions under which they will write a letter of referral for hormones or surgery clear, so that there are no surprises for the client as they plan their transition process. This transparency can help to repair the damage from past providers and build trust and rapport.

> Mental health conditions that are not reasonably well-controlled may prevent access to medical care

Another aspect of gatekeeping involves the use of assessments as a prerequisite for hormonal or surgical treatment. The financial costs associated with counseling and assessment can be onerous and burdensome for trans clients. If this type of care is covered by insurance, then it is possible the financial burden may not be a barrier for trans clients. However, there are a number of assessments that have wrongly been used to determine whether a trans person is "ready" for hormone treatment or surgical care. Personality assessments have been used for this purpose. Foremost among these is the Minnesota Multiphasic Personality Inventory–2 (MMPI-2; Butcher et al., 2001; The authors recognize that the MMPI-3 has been published. However, the MMPI-2 is the assessment tool that has been used for decades to determine readiness for transition. Readers are cautioned to not make the same mistakes with the MMPI-3).

> The use of psychological assessments for transition readiness is ill-advised

Like other personality assessments, the MMPI-2 requires the examiner to designate the sex of the examinee. Although arguments could be made for a number of ways to make this decision, the problem is that none of them is sufficient to acknowledge the lived experiences of trans people (Keo-Meier & Fitzgerald, 2017; NB: Colt Keo-Meier now uses the name Colt L. St. Amand). If you are using assessments for other means, such as in an intake evaluation or in therapy, providers will have to decide carefully how to use these tools. One argument would be to use the person's sex assigned at birth. A benefit of this approach is that it takes into consideration the gender expectations a person likely had to conform to as a child – in other words, it is the manner in which a person was socialized. This approach also has problems. For example, we know that children understand their gender identity at young ages. If a psychologist uses the sex a person was assigned at birth, they may ignore the fact that a client has held a different gender identity since early childhood. We will talk in greater detail about assessment later in this volume (see Section 3.1: Assessment).

There may be times when a client is not ready for hormones or surgical care. Informing them of this would not be gatekeeping. For instance, if a trans person is working to manage various social determinants of health (SDOH) such as homelessness and recent diagnosis of a disabling, chronic health condition, it may be appropriate to work with the client to help stabilize their life circumstances prior to initiating transition care. The reasoning for this is that a lack of stable housing may result in clients encountering issues in their recovery from surgery, for instance.

There are few, if any, mental health concerns that should lead a provider to withhold a letter of referral for care. This even includes severe depression (including suicidal ideation), hallucinations or other psychotic symptoms, and substance use disorders not preventing access to care. Even though these mental health concerns are considered to be serious, preventing a client from moving forward in their transition may exacerbate their mental health issues. The SOC (WPATH, 2012) state that any clinical concerns need to be reasonably well-controlled. Reasonably well-controlled is not defined in the SOC. This is explored in greater detail in Section 2.7.4: Reasonably Well-Controlled Mental Health.

Serious mental health concerns should not automatically lead to a denial of access to medical care

2

Theories and Models

It is important to honor a trans client's right to autonomy

At the core of affirming mental health services with trans clients is respect for the autonomy of trans individuals and their varied life and gender experiences (American Psychological Association [APA], 2015; Chang et al., 2018). Providers who adhere to these principles understand that there is no singular narrative for what it means to be trans and that trans people vary in their desires for socially, legally, or medically affirming their gender.

There are many ways for a trans person to affirm their gender

Furthermore, not all trans people socially, legally, or medically affirm their gender, for a variety of other reasons, such as safety concerns or difficulties accessing such services. In terms of clinical practice, there are three main treatment contexts in which providers serve trans clients: general mental health services, therapy related to supporting a person's gender exploration and affirmation, and clinical services targeted toward supporting clients in their medical gender affirmation process (e.g., providing letters of support, conducting evaluations for treatment [if needed], helping to address mental health challenges). These are not mutually exclusive and may overlap depending on the client.

The clinical concern for some trans clients may have nothing to do with their gender identity

In mental health services, clients may be seeking therapy due to any form of distress they are experiencing, such as depression or anxiety, as well as other life challenges (e.g., loss of employment, relationship concerns). Trans clients may be seeking therapy for reasons that are more closely connected to their experiences as trans individuals, such as managing stress around coming out and disclosing a trans identity, coping with social stigma, developing strategies for managing rejection from family, and other life challenges. More specifics about implementing an affirmative therapy approach are available in Section 4.2.1: Affirmative Practice.

Providers need to reflect on their own internalized understandings of gender

Here we describe the basic strategies that providers can implement to integrate a gender-affirming approach into their overall therapy services with trans clients given that many people may seek care unrelated to their gender experience. For starters, providers must understand that gender is a nonbinary construct, although most people have been socialized in a way that encourages binary thinking about gender and enforces this via policies, practices, gender norms, and physical manifestations of the gender binary (e.g., gendered restrooms, limited forms addressing sex/gender in applications; APA, 2015; Budge et al., 2014; Chang et al., 2018). Taking on this understanding of gender means that psychologists will need to unpack their own internalized understanding of gender and work through their assumptions of their own and others' gender experiences in order to provide an open space for clients to express and explore their gender without having psychologist-imposed expectations (Chang et al., 2018). This will influence the dialogue between psychologists and their clients as providers should ask about gender in an open-ended manner that does not assume a gender experience and explores the unique ways in which each client experiences and desires to express their gender (see Section 4.6 for information about interrogating your gender).

Our clients will learn very early in working with us whether we have an affirming and welcoming practice. Clients may find information about our clinical practice through an Internet search. Our websites serve as a glimpse into our thoughts about gender. Simple efforts such as listing your pronouns in your biography will help clients feel welcome.

Trans people will come to conclusions about our competence based on factors such as our website

Taking this one step further, use intake forms that allow the client the flexibility to use the terminology that best fits their identity. This can be challenging if you are using an electronic health record. It is becoming more common for electronic health records to include additional gender options beyond male and female. These are still limited, and clients should have the opportunity to use the language that best fits their identity. Making your paperwork available on your website will help clients to know that you have been reflective about ways to affirm their identities (if the paperwork is inclusive, of course). Past research has shown that providers who list themselves as being trans affirming, on websites like Psychology Today ("trans affirming" is a common search term when a person is looking for a provider) often do not take even the most basic steps that would indicate they are affirming of trans clients (Holt et al., 2018). We suggest that providers make explicit the actions they take to be affirming, so potential clients are empowered to make decisions about who to pursue care with. Being transparent about this also helps to ensure that competence and affirmation are more than words and are actually lived out in the work of providers.

Competence is much more than being an independently licensed provider

It is important that providers incorporate a strengths-based approach that empowers trans clients. A strengths-based approach can counter the social marginalization, discrimination, and violence that many trans clients may experience. Helping clients to identify positive traits, learning prosocial coping strategies, identifying the ways in which each client uniquely embodies resilience against oppression, and other strategies can assist the client as they work to manage day-to-day challenges. Psychologists can work with clients to develop skills that empower them to manage acts of oppression and help them to navigate oppressive contexts, such as problematic school environments, medical services, and legal systems. To utilize a strengths-based approach, providers may also benefit from learning about the unique experiences of resilience that manifest in the lives of trans people. Resilience for trans people can look like self-defining one's gender, community connectedness with other trans individuals, and developing critical consciousness about the systemic nature of oppression of trans people among others (Singh et al., 2011; see the subsection on resilience in Section 4.2.2: Therapeutic Approaches for more).

Clients may need support to develop skills to improve their resilience

2.1 Minority Stress Theory

A model that may help psychologists to understand and develop their case conceptualizations with clients is *minority stress theory* (MST; also termed *marginalization stress*; Brooks, 1981; Hendricks & Testa, 2012; Meyer, 2003;

> **Minority stress theory is a useful approach to conceptualizing a trans client's lived experience**

Testa et al., 2015). MST details the ways in which social marginalization comes to impact the mental health and well-being of marginalized groups. Originally developed with cisgender sexual minorities in mind, specifically lesbians and gay men (Brooks, 1981; Meyer, 2003), this model has been extended and adapted to better fit the experiences of trans individuals (Hendricks & Testa, 2012; Testa et al., 2015).

MST posits that people experience stressors from distal and proximal sources. Distal stressors are those that are overt or enacted. These stressors occur in a person's life because of bias and prejudice related to their trans identity. Examples might include discrimination or violence in the workplace (Hendricks & Testa, 2012; James et al., 2016). In response to an environment that is oppressive and marginalizing of trans people, individuals may also learn to expect rejection from others, conceal their identity, or may internalize this stigma (sometimes called *internalized transphobia* or *internalized cissexism*). When internalized, this stigma can manifest as negative views of oneself or others who are trans or as thoughts of self-hatred. In addition, trans people may find themselves on alert for mistreatment from others. They may display extraordinary vigilance in their day-to-day activities as a product of needing

> **Anticipation of stressors can have the effect of elevating baseline stress levels**

to be on watch for safety issues or other distal stressors. The anticipation of stressors can have a long-term impact on a person's sense of safety and well-being. It may also result in elevated levels of cortisol which can lead to myriad chronic health concerns. Overall, MST is helpful because it allows for an understanding of the causes of mental health disparities as socially embedded within sociopolitical contexts that are marginalizing and harmful to trans people. This shift in mindset is important for employing affirming treatment of trans clients rather than taking an individualistic perspective.

Testa and colleagues (2015) utilized MST for the purposes of developing the *Gender Minority Stress and Resilience Measure* (GMSRM). The GMSRM assesses the constructs of gender-related discrimination, gender-related rejec-

> **The GMSRM assesses minority stress and resilience and may be useful in clinical practice**

tion, gender-related victimization, nonaffirmation of gender identity, internalized transphobia, negative expectations for future events, nondisclosure, community connectedness, and pride. Testa and colleagues (2015) suggest that the measure is useful in clinical settings to "increase clinicians' and clients' awareness and understand[ing] of the unique risk and protective factors experienced" by trans people (p. 74). Psychologists are encouraged to employ this tool with their clients, as it may help bring greater awareness and understanding of the myriad difficulties trans people face. Some clinicians, especially those with a cisgender identity or those with little clinical experience, may benefit from this clinical picture.

2.1.1 Tailoring Minority Stress Theory to Trans People

> **MST was developed based on the experiences of cisgender sexual minorities and not trans people**

Even with this extension of MST, we believe that there are gaps in the framework, given the fact that this model originated with a focus on cisgender people (Puckett, 2019). Puckett and others (Rood et al., 2017) suggest that the proximal stressor of identity concealment can be very different for trans people.

Examples of this include the fact that a cisgender, sexual minority may be able to conceal their sexual identity with relative ease. Trans people do not always have this ability. This happens as a person makes a medical transition and begins to experience changes to secondary sex characteristics (e.g., voice pitch for trans masculine people, tracheal shave for a trans feminine person). Some trans people never publicly disclose their gender identity (this is known as being *stealth* or as *woodworking*). Although this may create a sense of safety, the trans person may also be concerned that someone will learn of their gender history. Notably, for trans people what has traditionally been called identity concealment may refer to a person not disclosing to others a trans identity when initially faced with coming out to others, or it could refer to someone not sharing their gender history and that they have affirmed their gender in the past. Some trans people may not want others to know about their transition history and this nondisclosure could be an act of self-affirmation. It is important to understand the function of not disclosing or revealing one's trans history rather than to inherently view this negatively or as a stressor.

Puckett (2019) includes the following as possible minority stressors: misgendering, nonaffirmation, vicarious exposure to stress narratives, and heightened vigilance regarding the possibility of encountering minority stress. As outlined in Table 2, there are a variety of stressors with which a provider should be familiar. Learning about these can facilitate a nuanced understanding of clients' experiences and help to inform the case conceptualization that guides treatment (Appendix 1). Notably, exploring stressors and listening for these in the narratives of clients help to understand clients' lived experiences from a contextualized, person-centered perspective. Broadly speaking, providers can keep this model in mind in their clinical practice to guide their understanding of trans clients' mental health. This helps providers to ensure that they are not pathologizing trans clients and are understanding the contextual and social factors that may drive mental health outcomes in trans communities. Using a MST-informed practice can shape the treatment plan as psychologists are able to identify specific treatment targets (e.g., internalized stigma) and help clients to develop the critical consciousness necessary for decreasing self-blame.

> When and how trans people share their gender history may be different from one person to another

> Trans people face numerous challenges with which providers should be familiar

Table 2
Stressors and marginalization in the trans community

Type of marginalization stress	Definition	Example
Enacted stigma	Overt acts of oppression and bias against trans individuals, such as discrimination, harassment, and violence.	A trans man being fired from his job after refusing to use the women's restroom.
Internalized stigma	When trans people come to develop negative views about themselves and/or other trans people due to social stigma of trans identities.	A trans client who expresses shame about their gender identity and blames themselves for others' biases.

Table 2. Continued

Type of marginalization stress	Definition	Example
Expectations of rejection	Anticipating that others will not be accepting of trans people.	A nonbinary client who expresses a lot of worry and fear about disclosing their pronouns to others.
Identity concealment	Not disclosing a trans identity or history (note. this may or may not be stressful – some trans people view nondisclosure as an act of self-affirmation).	A genderfluid client who has not come out to anyone yet and only dresses in affirming ways in the privacy of their room and expresses high amounts of stress related to the misgendering experienced on a daily basis.
Misgendering	Reference to trans people in ways that differ from or negate their current gender identity.	A trans woman being referred to as "Sir."
Sociopolitical stressors	Events and legal or political actions that are marginalizing of trans individuals.	A trans person's state legislature proposing a law that would require people to use the restroom associated with their sex assigned at birth on their original birth certificate.
Vicarious stress	The emotional toll of exposure to stress narratives from other trans people or social representations of trans people.	A genderqueer person turning on the news and hearing about two recent murders of trans people of color.
Limited future orientation	Feeling that one's future is limited either in quality or time due to the oppression trans people experience and the social narratives about trans lives.	A nonbinary client who feels that their life circumstances will never improve due to living in a rural area with high levels of stigma.
Bodily vigilance	Feeling as if one's body and gender is being monitored by others.	A trans man who reports feeling nervous when shopping in the men's section due to glances from others and comments on his appearance.

2.1.2 Suicide and Minority Stress

MST has been applied to understanding suicide and suicide ideation in trans people (Tebbe & Moradi, 2016; Testa et al., 2017). Important in this work is the understanding that the sources of stress experienced by trans people can be triggers for suicidal thoughts and behavior. Studies have shown suicide attempt rates in the trans community to be over 40% (James et al., 2016). This number is representative of trans people who reported having attempted suicide at least once in their lifetime. If a psychologist wants to work with trans people and do so in a manner that is culturally competent, they must be able to talk with depressed trans clients about risk and protective factors related to suicide. Not doing so and not being able to ask a client about their suicide risk is an egregious treatment omission that may be associated with fatal consequences.

Suicide attempt rates in the trans community are alarmingly high and represent a public health crisis

Tebbe and Moradi (2016) found that depression mediated the association between perceived experiences of discrimination, fear of antitrans stigma, and friend support with suicide risk. In other words, depression helped explain the relationship to suicide risk. As a psychologist works with their client, they should attend to symptoms of depression and to experiences of mistreatment. Tebbe and Moradi also found that drugs (but not alcohol) are associated with suicide risk. These findings were consistent across gender identities.

Drug use, but not alcohol, in trans people may be a risk factor for suicidal behavior

In another study, Testa and colleagues (2017) applied MST and interpersonal theory to understand how the integration of these theories explain suicidal ideation and attempts in trans people. Results indicated that rejection, nonaffirmation, and victimization were related to suicidal ideation as influenced by internalized transphobia and negative expectations of rejection. Testa and colleagues (2017) also found that internalized transphobia and negative expectations influenced suicidal ideation, when the concepts of thwarted belongingness and perceived burdensomeness (concepts from interpersonal theory) were considered.

Even though MST was originally conceptualized for the impacts it had on cisgender sexual minorities, it is clear from extant research that it also impacts trans people's lives, as seen above in the examples about suicidality. As will be discussed later (see Section 4.1.1: Specific Clinical Concerns), mood disorders, including major depression, are relatively common for trans people. There are times, indeed, when that is the presenting clinical concern. Psychologists must know of the ways that other challenges that trans people face might complicate depression and therefore increase suicide risk.

MST helps to explain suicide risk in trans people

2.2 Gender Dysphoria

The current diagnostic label for people who are experiencing distress from their physical appearance or gender characteristics not aligning with their gender identity is *gender dysphoria* (American Psychiatric Association, 2013). Some version of this disorder has been present in the DSM since the DSM-III-R. The DSM-III-R was also the first printed version of the DSM that did not include homosexuality as a mental disorder (although remnants of this diagnosis remained in sections like the "Sexual Disorders Not Otherwise Specified" for many years to follow). Some people believed that the presence of gender identity disorder (the name used at the time) was an attempt to identify individuals who would later come to identify as sexual minorities (lesbian, gay, bisexual, or other nonheterosexual people) as it was thought that gender nonconformity was a marker of this later sexual identification. The term for this was *pre-homosexual*. At the time, the use of conversion or reparative therapies was common for gay, lesbian, bisexual, queer, and other nonheterosexual people. Although conversion therapy was also used for trans people, it has only been in recent years that this type of treatment has been broadly criticized. Conversion therapy is considered harmful and unethical today (APA, 2021; Substance Abuse Mental Health Services Administration [SAMHSA], 2015). Conversion therapy will be discussed in further detail in Section 4.7.1.

> Providers engaging in conversion therapy may be harming their patients

In the DSM-IV and the DSM-IV-TR there was a diagnosis of *gender identity disorder*. Members of the trans community have protested the use of mental health disorders to classify their experiences. There have been numerous concerns expressed, including that the diagnosis inherently pathologized trans individuals' identities, even in the name. Another concern was related to the need to specify a person's sexual orientation. At the time, a psychologist could add a specifier that a trans person was attracted to men, women, both, or neither. There was no need for this specification outside of identifying sexual minorities, which is likely connected to the history outlined in the SOC, where trans people were expected to have a heterosexual orientation posttransition. People are critical of the placement of this entity within the DSM. Gender identity disorder was included in a section that included sexual disorders (e.g., vaginismus, erectile dysfunction) and paraphilias (e.g., pedophilia, voyeurism). In 2013, the DSM-5 was published. In this version, the disorder is named "gender dysphoria," and it is in a section by itself. Other changes include the removal of the sexual orientation specifiers. The diagnostic criteria have not changed substantially.

> The diagnosis of gender dysphoria may be necessary depending on a client's transition goals

In the DSM-5 (American Psychiatric Association, 2013), the criteria for gender dysphoria in adolescents and adults was changed little from the previous version of the DSM. According to these criteria, trans people need to endorse there being a mismatch between their felt gender and the sex they were assigned at birth. This needs to have been present for at least 6 months and may manifest as a desire to be rid of primary or secondary sex characteristics or to have the primary or secondary sex characteristics of another gender. The language in criterion A is written such that people with nonbinary identities may also be diagnosed. As is true for most disorders in the DSM, there needs to be clinically significant distress across one or more domains of a person's life. There are also specifiers for clients who have a difference of sex development or if the client is described as "post-transition," meaning that they are living in their affirmed gender and have received some form of medical care to affirm their gender (or are preparing to do so). The medical care can include hormones or surgery to affirm clients' genders.

> Talking with your client about diagnosis and what it means for them may reduce the client's stress

There remains controversy within the trans community about the usefulness of this diagnosis. On the one hand, trans people are not happy that they need to be diagnosed with a mental health diagnosis to receive coverage for gender-affirming medical care. Furthermore, if a trans person is experiencing distress, there is a good chance it is related to the ways the individual experiences discrimination and other types of mistreatment.

On the other hand, trans activists say that the presence of the diagnosis makes it possible to access care for those who are most marginalized. For instance, if a person has been incarcerated, they need the diagnosis to be able to access hormones or surgery. The same is true for people on Medicare (e.g., people over the age of 65 or someone with a disability) or Medicaid (e.g., people living in poverty and children). Although coverage of care for trans people is inconsistent if a person is on Medicare or Medicaid, they certainly will not be able to access medical treatment if they do not have a diagnosis or if the care is not considered to be medically necessary.

2.2.1 Reclassifying Gender Dysphoria

Recently, the WHO (n.d.) decided to move the gender dysphoria diagnosis from the mental health chapters of the ICD-11 to a medical chapter, and it is now identified as a sexual health concern (WHO, n.d.). In addition to the change in location, the disorder will be renamed as *gender incongruence*. It took a very long time for the US to begin the use of ICD-10. Hopefully, it will not take as long to adopt the ICD-11.

> Gender incongruence is a new term that has replaced gender dysphoria in the ICD

Moving the disorder out of the mental health chapters may lend additional credibility to the idea that any treatment is medically necessary, although the inclusion in the sexual health chapter may be complicated, as this could be viewed as an inappropriate location. Regardless, medical designation of dysphoria (or incongruence) is often required by insurance companies to cover the costs of treatment. Trans people and mental health professionals are faced with how to facilitate access to care in the least stigmatizing way possible.

Ultimately, it would be most useful for our trans clients and their providers if the placement of the disorder was consistent across diagnostic tools. This would ensure consistency with regard to the criteria associated with gender dysphoria. Insurance companies would also benefit from this consistency.

2.3 Medical Necessity

Every year, more insurance companies and employers are covering medical care related to trans health. Historically, the city of San Francisco was the first city to cover the costs of hormone treatment and surgical care for trans employees (Human Rights Campaign, n.d.). This began in 2001.

> Medical necessity is a phrase that is often required when a trans person is accessing medical treatment

The decision to cover trans health was controversial. Even so, the coverage limits were such that there was not a significant amount of coverage. There was a lifetime limit of US $50,000. All city of San Francisco employees paid an additional $1.70 per month to help cover this care. Within 3 years, the city had accumulated $4.3 million in surcharge payments and had only paid out $156,000 in claims. The lifetime limit was increased to $75,000, and the surcharge was decreased to $0.50. After 5 years, the city had $5.6 million from the surcharge payments and had paid out a total of just over $383,000. From

Claims for San Francisco were much lower than expected and led to dropping surcharges and limits

that point forward, the city stopped collecting the surcharge. Lifetime caps have been eliminated by insurance providers offering coverage for city of San Francisco employees. This is true for other health plans due to the changes in the Affordable Care Act which made it illegal to discriminate in health care coverage on the basis of gender (US Department of Health and Human Services [DHHS], 2021).

The information from the claims' performance was useful for other employers, as they considered whether to offer this type of health care protection for their employees. The costs for care can vary significantly. Hormone treatment is likely to last the rest of a person's life, but it is the least expensive aspect of medical care. Most expensive are the costs associated with genital surgery for people who were AFAB. Genital surgery for trans men costs easily well over US $100,000 and typically involves multiple surgeries.

In 2015, the DHHS proposed a rule (known as Section 1557) that would make it categorically illegal to discriminate against trans people in the delivery of health care (DHHS, 2021). This means that it would be against the law for most insurance providers to say that they would not cover any transition-related care. This has been changed to state that most insurance carriers cannot deny a specific type of care.

Treatment for gender affirmation is medically necessary care

Another important change over time has been that most insurance providers can no longer place lifetime caps on coverage if that cap would be discriminatory toward trans people. However, if the care that trans people want or need to access is not considered to be medically necessary, they will not be able to get the care covered through any health insurance plan. Most major professional health care organizations, including the APA (2008), have made clear statements about the ways that trans health care is medically necessary. An insurance carrier is not going to cover medical treatment (including mental health treatment) that is not medically necessary. The problem has been that some treatment that trans people require is considered to be cosmetic. Procedures that may be classified as cosmetic may include, but are not limited to, facial feminization, feminization laryngoplasty, voice therapy, and hair transplants. What should be noted is that each of the aforementioned procedures would be sought by trans feminine people. There are some procedures that trans masculine people may not be able to access (e.g., infertility treatments), and most of these will also be a difficult health concern for trans feminine people too. If you were to ask your trans client if these treatments were medically necessary, the answer would likely be "absolutely!" However, insurance carriers are the ones who decide whether to cover a medical procedure. As a result, some care that trans people want to access is not covered and therefore is not within reach.

Trans people may have to submit multiple appeals before they are able to get coverage

As a psychologist, you may be asked to write a letter in support of a trans person as they attempt to access medical care. It is critical that the text of the letter include that the treatment for which you are making a referral is medically necessary. Failure to do so may lead to the denial of coverage for care. A trans client may then have to engage in multiple appeals to ensure that they are able to access care. The appeal process can be lengthy and challenging.

2.4 Informed Consent

Mental health providers have historically been placed in the gatekeeping role in working with trans clients who are seeking medical care for gender affirmation (Ashley, 2019). There are approaches that are viewed more positively among trans individuals. Some medical providers have adopted an informed consent approach in providing hormone therapy, such as the Howard Brown Health Center in Chicago (https://howardbrown.org/). Using this approach, the provider conducts a brief assessment to ensure that the client can provide *consent* and is *informed* about the effects of hormones and their potential side effects. Clients who are deemed able to provide consent for these services are given access to care (Schulz, 2018). For surgical means of affirming one's gender, an evaluation is typically required from a mental health professional.

Informed consent is used to enable access to hormones more often than for surgical treatments

There are many medical providers that still require a letter of support from a psychologist for hormone therapy. Mental health providers need to ensure they are approaching their evaluations or assessments in a way that honors their clients' autonomy and ability to make choices about their care, rather than increasing barriers to services or approaching their work from misguided assumptions that their role is to evaluate the authenticity of a trans person's identity. Assuming that the provider is the one who can determine whether a trans person's identity is authentic can be considered an abuse of power. It is the trans person who understands their sense of self.

Our trans clients understand their identities and are most knowledgeable about their needs

Another problem with the assumption that the provider is the expert, is that it is possible that the psychologist will have inaccurate beliefs about a trans person's experience of gender identity. There are many paths that a trans person may take in realizing, disclosing, and affirming their gender identity. Trans people do not need their mental health provider to define that for them.

An affirming approach to a mental health evaluation includes sharing your views on gender with clients and being transparent in the evaluation process to ensure that clients know what to anticipate. Notably, an evaluation is different from providing therapy, and trans clients are not required to go to therapy to obtain letters of support for their gender-affirming medical care. Psychologists should complete the evaluation in an efficient manner, help ensure the client has the information necessary to make a decision about their care, assess for other mental health conditions that may impact decision making or capacity to consent, and evaluate the client's overall ability to provide consent. This information is needed for the letter that is provided to the client, to the client's medical provider, or to the insurance company. Information about letter writing is provided in Section 4.3: Variations of the Method: Letter Writing. The section includes specifics of the therapeutic encounter and how to address the necessary language for letters of referral.

Counseling is not required for trans people who are seeking a letter of referral for care

2.5 Harm Reduction

Some clients may secure hormones through friends or outside of medical settings, and this has the potential to be dangerous. The danger arises because the client may not know if the hormones are from a safe source. Providers can

> **There are many ways psychologists can advocate for clients, including access to safe healthcare**

help reduce the risk clients face by helping them connect to affirming medical providers. In this situation, psychologists can act as advocates for their clients by ensuring clients have information about providers who are affirming and by assisting them through the process of obtaining medical care (see Appendix 2). In using a harm reduction approach to treatment, the provider will ensure that the client continues to have access to hormones and that the hormones are secured from a safe source. Clients may also need assistance advocating for themselves if their medical provider does not take a harm reduction approach or if the provider denies the client services. Broadly, we know that when there are barriers to affirming one's gender, a client is likely to feel increased levels of distress. Research shows that affirming one's gender through medical means (if this is desired by the person) is associated with mental health improvements (Keo-Meier et al., 2015). It is important that medical providers take a harm reduction approach that prioritizes the health and well-being of the client and does not add additional barriers to their care including logistical and financial costs.

2.6 Shaping the Therapeutic Dialogue

In many ways, working with trans clients is no different from working with cisgender clients. You will begin with an intake session. This will allow you to gain a better understanding of the reasons the client is seeking help. From there, you will develop a treatment plan. This should be a collaborative effort with your client. From there, you should engage in evidence-based practices with your clients. Eventually you will discuss termination and ending therapy once goals are achieved.

Although this seems basic, it takes only a simple misstep for things to go awry. The following are recommended interactions when beginning work with a trans person. This is not intended to be an exhaustive list of dialogue prompts. It should provide some direction for the most basic ways you can communicate with your client. In addition, we suggest that you engage in critical self-reflection on your work as a provider working with trans clients (see Section 4.6: Importance of Interrogating Your Gender). Unpacking the ways that cisnormativity shapes all of our views is a lifelong process. We suggest that you regularly make attempts to reflect on your practice, seek continuing education from reputable sources, and continue growing in these areas. You also might find tools, such as the Trans-Inclusive Provider Scale by Kattari et al. (2020), a useful way to identify areas for improvement or a helpful prompt for areas for self-reflection. Figure 1 provides an overview of actions and strategies to demonstrate cultural responsivity and affirmation of trans clients' experiences.

> **Cisnormativity leads to the devaluing of trans people and assumptions that everyone is cisgender**

2.6.1 Introducing Yourself With Your Pronoun(s)

One of the ways trans people are invalidated is when another person misgenders them. When you introduce yourself with your pronouns, you are sending a signal to your client that you understand the importance of pronouns which

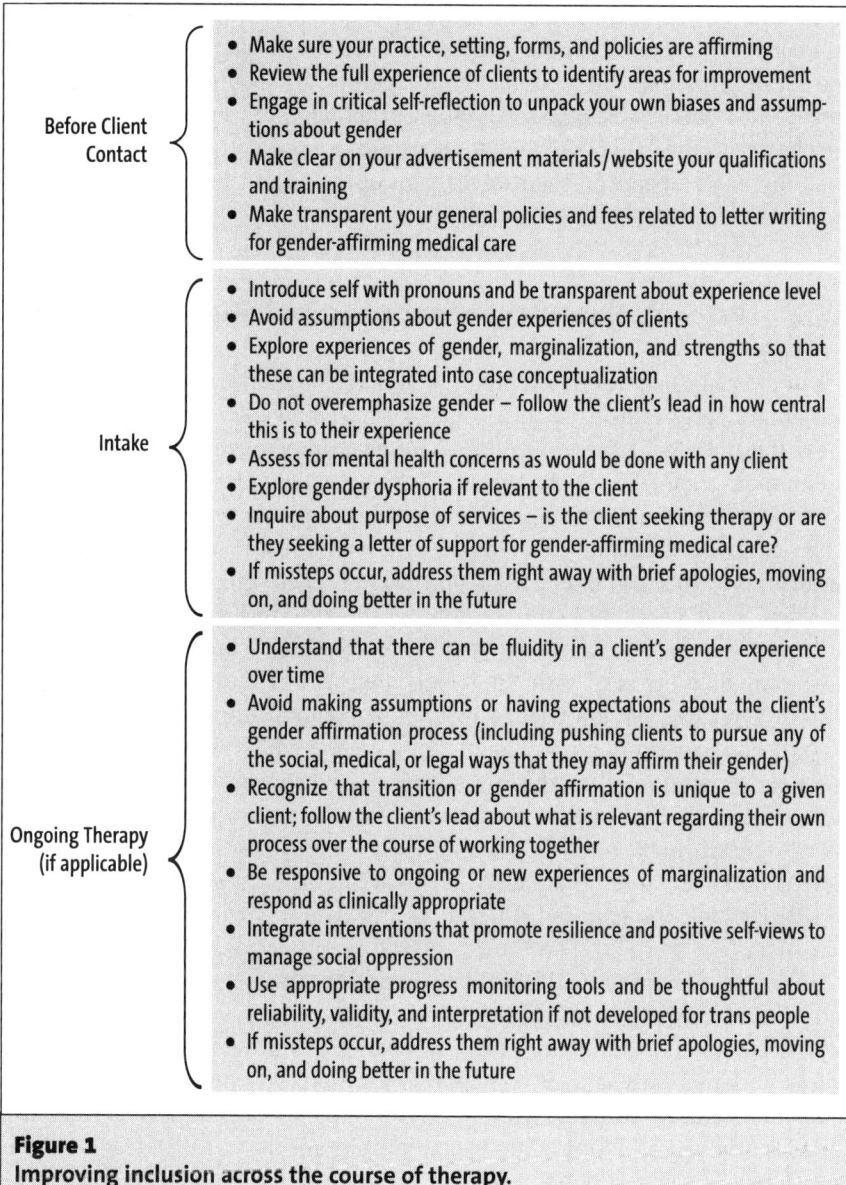

Figure 1
Improving inclusion across the course of therapy.

are deeply linked to gender. For instance, one could say "Hello, I'm Dr. Jae Puckett and my pronouns are they/them." This simple act can be a source of relief for your client as they enter a clinical relationship with you and provides an opening for clients to share their pronouns with you with less fear about broaching the topic. We recommend that you introduce yourself with your pronouns to all clients, not just those you know to be trans or who you think could be. If you go the latter route, you may be making inaccurate assumptions about your new clients. We do not know another person's pronouns until they share them with us.

Pronouns are very personal, and asking your client about the pronouns they use can help to build the foundation of trust in the clinical relationship. Like

> Introduce yourself with your pronouns and invite clients to share their pronouns as well

other aspects of a trans person's identity, your clients may shift their use of pronouns. For example, some people may start exploring their gender using one set of pronouns and then change to another. As they come to understand their gender this may change. Although pronouns used by nonbinary people may be unfamiliar, it is critical that you make every effort to use the pronouns your clients are using for themselves. Not doing so can lead to difficulties in the clinical relationship.

2.6.2 Presentation of Experience and Training

Clients should be able to easily identify your training and qualifications to work with trans people

It is not very typical for a psychologist to describe their training in-depth to a new client. Part of this is because when we see a new client, we do not always know their clinical concern (unless there has already been an intake session within their organization). As a generalist, you may not have an area of expertise or specialization. As discussed elsewhere in this volume (see Section 4.1.1: Specific Clinical Concerns), some trans people will come for care because of mental health concerns that are unrelated to their gender identity.

Even so, if you know you are going to be working with a trans client, it is helpful for them to know that you have committed the time necessary to have more than the very basic knowledge that was obtained while in graduate school. Typically, the knowledge from your doctoral training will be limited to what you learned in a psychopathology course with a focus on the DSM-5 or an earlier edition of it. This knowledge is insufficient and is likely to create a rift between you and a trans client, because it is very limited and does not recognize the many ways a trans person experiences their gender. Further, there is no information in the DSM-5 (let alone earlier editions) that will help you understand the nuanced differences between a social, legal, or medical transition.

Expertise in diagnosis is not sufficient to call yourself an expert in care for trans people

In the past, training in affirmative work with trans people was hard to find and came at a significant cost. At this time, organizations such as the American Psychological Association and PESI have multiple programs that are easy to access in digital formats (see Appendix 3 for more information about training sources). Training programs can be 1-hour sessions or multiday events. The WPATH has been offering a multisession program that will lead to certification (https://www.wpath.org/gei). This program is designed to recognize the training and experience a provider might have that allows a path to certification for providers who have been working in the field for 10 or more years.

Trans clients should not be expected to educate their providers

Cultural and clinical competency is not simply a preferred approach to psychological work. It is an ethical mandate. One of the common narratives from trans people is that their providers expect the client to educate them about the experiences of trans people. It is certainly acceptable to ask your clients about their own life, but asking them about more basic information is unacceptable. Trained psychologists would never expect a client with depression or anxiety to provide education or make recommendations for clinical approaches to treatment for these experiences. As such, when a client is presenting with gender dysphoria, psychologists should not rely on the client to educate them about this either.

2.6.3 Avoid Assumptions About What an Identity Term Means for the Client

It is very easy to make inaccurate assumptions when working with a trans client. The first author of this present volume worked with a trans feminine client and the only thing he knew about the client was that she was interested in undergoing surgery. The first author mistakenly assumed that the client was interested in genital surgery. The client very quickly corrected this mistake by stating that "oh no, my business down there isn't going anywhere" (see Section 2.6.6: How to Respond When You Make a Mistake).

This type of mistake is easy to make, as people may have fixed ideas about the reasons a trans person might be seeking counseling or engaging in a transition. In some ways, the assumptions that we make about others may be based on inaccurate stereotypes. Examples of these stereotypes include assuming that a trans person (a) has a binary gender identity, (b) identifies with the lesbian, gay, bisexual, transgender, and queer (LGBTQ+) movement, (c) wants to access hormones and surgery, (d) experiences discrimination and violence based on their gender, (e) knew from early childhood that their sex assigned at birth was not consistent with their felt gender, (f) had experiences in childhood that were more like a child of the "opposite sex," (g) will leave the relationship they are in or will be unable to find a partner and will be single for the rest of their life, or (h) that trans people of color will be living with HIV as a result of having engaged in sex work.

Stereotypes about trans people can be very harmful when psychologists fail to listen to their clients

Stereotypes about trans people may intersect with other identities, like race

There are often assumptions that trans people broadly fall into "binary" and "nonbinary" experiences, yet the actual experiences of many trans people are more nuanced. For instance, a person who may identify specifically as a trans man, may also identify with other terms like "genderflux" or a combination of gender terms. Simply knowing a term does not mean that providers should then assume they understand the client's gender experience.

2.6.4 Trans Client Fluidity in Their Gender and Sexuality

Gender identity and sexual orientation can be fluid for some trans people. The old narrative that a trans person would be heterosexual posttransition was not created by trans people. Rather, providers would not allow a person to transition if their identity posttransition would lead to a same-sex/gender relationship. There is a growing body of research exploring sexuality in trans people (dickey et al., 2012; Fox Tree-McGrath et al., 2018). Additionally, regardless of the age of the client you are working with, it is possible that a trans client will shift their gender identity, the pronoun(s) they use, and their name. Failure to keep up with these changes will likely lead to a clinical rupture. It is the task of therapists to create a clinical relationship that invites clients to share this information should it change over time.

Fluidity can be common for some trans people

2.6.5 Avoid Assumptions About Transition

Assumptions, like stereotypes, can be dangerous when working with trans people

Trans clients may engage in more than one type of transition. Historically, it was assumed there was only a medical transition. As of this writing, a transition may be social, legal, or medical (see the entry for "Transition," in Section 1.2, for more information about transition types). Further, the way one trans person makes a social transition may be very different from the way another person does. We must be very deliberate in asking our clients what a transition means for them. Explaining why you are asking about what transition means to the client may help them be less likely to become suspicious of needing to educate their provider. In the same ways that depression or anxiety may be different for two people, so too can gender identity and sexual orientation.

Nonbinary identities are no less legitimate than other trans identities

We encourage providers to reflect on any internalized stereotypes or expectations for clients in terms of gender affirmation, identity, or expression. Providers may assume that trans women and trans men will want to pursue all available medical forms of gender affirmation and that other trans individuals such as people who are genderqueer, nonbinary, or agender would not wish to do so. These types of assumptions are dangerous, as they can lead to a rupture of the therapeutic relationship, displays of microaggressions in session with clients, and problematic gatekeeping practices, such as questioning the legitimacy of a nonbinary individual's pursuits of medical gender affirmation. There is great variability across trans people when it comes to their desire to pursue gender-affirming medical care and regarding having the means to pursue this care.

2.6.6 How to Respond When You Make a Mistake

Mistakes are bound to happen – think ahead as to how you will handle them

It is not a matter of whether you will make a mistake with a trans client but rather when. As important as recognizing having made a mistake, is the way in which you apologize for having done so. When a psychologist fails to apologize for having made a mistake with pronouns or the client's name, for example, it is then the responsibility of the client to correct the provider or to sacrifice their self by swallowing the discomfort of not bringing it up at all. Given the power dynamic that is inherent in a clinical relationship, a client may not feel safe correcting their provider. The more often the client feels as though they need to correct their provider, the less likely it is that they will feel safe and understood.

Keeping apologies short is one way to ensure that you do not make the situation worse

When you make a mistake, it is important to acknowledge the mistake, apologize for what you did or said, and truly work to ensure the mistake does not happen again. This process should not take long. It can be just as awkward for the client if the provider offers a long-winded explanation about why they made the mistake and the ways that this will continue to be hard for them. This type of apology is dismissive and indicates the provider's inability to see the client and respect their identity. Keep apologies short and to the point.

2.6.7 Understanding Diverse Experiences of Gender

One of the core aspects of engaging in affirming work with trans clients is to understand that gender is diverse, and there is no singular way to experience one's gender or to be trans. Socially, there are often very restrictive narratives about gender identity development for trans individuals. These narratives emphasize knowing from an early age that a person identifies as trans and undergoing various steps of medical transition. Although this narrative fits for some trans people's experiences, it does not fit for every trans person. Some trans people do not recognize their gender questions or identity early in their life and may not come to this awareness or find the language to describe their experiences until later in life. Individuals who do not fit this restrictive, narrow understanding of trans people's experiences are no less valid in their experiences as trans people, and providers must honor their client's individual experiences rather than relying on rigid, inaccurate stereotypes.

To understand what gender identity means for your clients, listen to their story

Providers must recognize that gender experiences are diverse across trans people and that trans people may identify in ways that fall outside of the identities of men and women. This is embedded within the practice guidelines from the American Psychological Association (APA, 2015), which state that psychologists should understand that gender is not binary and respect the range of identities that exist. Taking an approach that is open to the varied experiences of trans individuals empowers clients to share their authentic experiences with providers, helps to build rapport, and will help providers to more accurately understand their clients' experiences and thus provide stronger clinical care.

2.6.8 Review the Client Experience in Your Practice

Take time to review the experiences clients have at your practice to ensure that you are taking the necessary steps to provide an affirming experience. You should critically evaluate the full range of experiences clients have with your clinic, starting with how referrals are made or the first points of contact with receptionists, to identify areas for improvement. For instance, there can be subtle displays of cisnormativity in interpersonal interactions, such as assuming what gendered terms fit for a person based on voice over the phone (e.g., using the terms "Ma'am" or "Sir" on the phone with a client contacting your clinic for an intake instead of refraining from using gendered terms). Instead, use gender neutral terms or use the client's name. As such, it is essential that providers ensure that members of their staff are aware of the ways this type of interaction can happen and to identify any changes needed to decrease the likelihood of microaggressions (or worse) happening to clients.

In addition, providers should locate a gender-neutral restroom in their practice. It is unreasonable for trans-affirming providers to believe that clients can come to their office yet not be given access to a restroom (if they are not comfortable in gendered restrooms), when cisgender people are not faced with this dilemma. Lack of access to restrooms is associated with health complications, such as kidney infections, as well as less engagement in one's life, such as limiting public outings or restricting water and food intake. A psychologist's

Making sure that you have safe spaces for trans clients to use a restroom is essential

office should not be a space that brings on these concerns that plague other areas of trans people's lives.

Subtle messages about gender are also communicated through the written materials and readings that providers have available in their waiting rooms, as well as artwork. Providers should ensure that trans people are represented in these materials and may want to consider displaying other signs of inclusivity such as a trans pride flag sticker. Although a small indication of efforts to be inclusive, some trans people may look for signs like these to let them know that their providers are making an effort to be inclusive and affirming of trans individuals.

2.6.9 Knowledge of Local Resources

Trans clients may need help securing resources and navigating referrals. It will benefit your clients if you are already prepared and have done research about referrals that are of a good quality. In conducting your own research, make sure that the resources you suggest to trans clients are actually affirming and helpful. It is not uncommon for trans clients to receive referrals only to find that these resources hold problematic views of trans people or are not entirely affirming or competent. Following up with resources that are reported to be problematic based on the client's experience shows your commitment to engaging in an affirmative practice. The following is a list of items you should include when creating a resource list (note that this list is not intended to be exhaustive):

Knowledge of affirming referrals can help clients get their needs met

- Local LGBTQ+ community centers
- Support groups for trans individuals (with attention to subgroups that may align to certain identities, e.g., nonbinary or trans masculine people)
- Support groups for families of trans individuals
- Hotlines and online supports for trans individuals that address the need for crisis response
- Social groups that emphasize community building and connections with other trans individuals
- Places to buy gender-affirming gear and clothing (whether a brick-and-mortar location or an online resource)
- Businesses that are affirming that provide electrolysis or laser hair removal
- Other mental health providers and psychiatrists (including those who accept clients with Medicaid or Medicare)
- Medical providers for general health care services
- Medical providers for hormone therapy services (which may be the same as general health care services)
- Surgeons for gender-affirming procedures
- Gynecological and reproductive health care providers (including sperm banks)
- Information on state-level policies regarding name and gender marker changes
- Inpatient units, treatment centers, and other health care facilities and their policies on housing for trans clients

- Conferences that are specifically for members of the trans community (see Appendix 7)
- Shelters for people who are experiencing a housing crisis and their policies about how to house trans people
- Sporting and cultural activities that are known to be trans-welcoming

Through establishing such a list, psychologists will be prepared to make suggestions and referrals to clients whenever the need arises.

2.7 Nuanced Clinical Topics

Trans people are often required to seek care from psychologists or other mental health providers. The main reason this happens is because one or more of the trans client's providers has requested a letter of referral from a mental health provider. We will focus on specific treatment approaches in Chapter 4. Here, we address several clinical concerns that may not come up. Trans people deserve to have care from providers who understand these nuanced and often-avoided topics.

2.7.1 Grief

There are many positive and empowering shifts that happen in trans people's lives as they come out and affirm their gender. Even so, this time of change may also be accompanied with other feelings like grief for some trans people. Grief is a normal reaction people have at a time when they have experienced a significant loss or change. When a trans person makes a transition, there are a number of ways they may experience loss and change. Losses might include relationships (intimate or otherwise), employment, housing, or access to education. Even though the changes can be welcomed by a trans person, the individual may still have difficulty with the feelings of grief. In the past, providers have indicated to their trans patients that if they experience grief then they are not "really trans." This type of response oversimplifies the nature of a transition and is harmful for clients.

Trans people may experience losses across several domains of their life

Grief is not limited to the response a person has to another person's death or a relationship break-up. Talking about grief will allow the client to address their feelings and to normalize the grief process. If you are prepared to have this discussion with your client, you will be ready to address the concerns when they arise. In not being ready to have this discussion, you may be sending the message that there is something wrong with having a grief reaction. This can lead a trans person to avoid addressing any grief and loss they may be experiencing. In the end, trans clients are the ones who suffer if their provider holds the expectation that grief is inappropriate.

In the research literature, most studies explore the losses that parents experience when their child or adolescent transitions. Although this is important for those psychologists who work with families, it is not the same as the loss and grief a trans person experiences. In one of the only publications found, Kashubeck-West and colleagues (2017) explore the losses a trans person might face if they decide to leave a religious organization they belong to. This loss is not insignificant for many people. They may have belonged to a particular faith tradition most of their lives and suddenly find that coming out as a trans person is antithetical to the beliefs they previously held. It is this type of experience that trans people may face and struggle to manage.

2.7.2 Suicide and Trans People

Trans people likely have the highest rates of suicide attempts of any marginalized group of people in the US. Unfortunately, data about attempts and completions are not tracked by any governmental organization, including the Centers for Disease Control and Prevention. These high rates of suicide attempts are a public health concern (dickey & Budge, 2020).

> It is important that providers be prepared to discuss suicidality with clients

Studies have reported that 40% or more of trans participants have attempted suicide at least once in their lifetime (James et al., 2016). Although the results of these studies were part of community surveys, the research team included respected researchers. It is important to ask trans clients about suicidal thoughts and behaviors, without assuming this is part of their history, but instead creating avenues for clients to bring this up when necessary.

In Section 2.7.4: Reasonably Well-Controlled Mental Health, we will explore the concept of reasonably well-controlled and its significance in working with trans people. The presence of suicidal thoughts or behaviors may not be a contraindication to readiness for hormones or surgery. Any time a client reports suicidality, a provider should conduct a thorough risk assessment. If your client is not in imminent danger, and you feel certain that they have the necessary support systems in place, there may not be a reason to withhold the initiation of a social, medical, or legal transition. Some people think that pausing or stopping a trans person from moving forward will provide more time to work through emotional challenges. Others, and this is what we recommend, believe that trans clients likely have a good sense for what they can or cannot manage. The client's desire to transition or their felt sense that they are a gender different from the sex assigned at birth is not likely to be the source of depressive symptoms. Rather, it is the myriad ways that trans people experience mistreatment, discrimination, and violence in their daily lives that is potentially influencing their emotional state.

> Feelings of meaninglessness, helplessness, hopelessness, and an inability to cope may indicate suicide risk

As mentioned in Section 2.6.9: Knowledge of Local Resources, having a list of resources for clients who are at risk of suicidal thoughts or behaviors will allow the client to have sufficient support when they become most hopeless, such as through increasing their social networks via support groups. Woodrum and colleagues (2021) found an important link with demoralization and suicidal risk. Demoralization is conceptualized as the "persistent inability to cope and a profound sense of helplessness, hopelessness, and meaninglessness" (D. M. Clarke & Kissane, 2002, p. 733). Understanding suicide through the lens of demoralization can help providers explore the client's experiences with suicidal ideation and behaviors. It can be the case that a trans person has no idea of where they can get support. This may lead to what feels like a never-ending loop for a trans person. They do not know where to find an affirming provider, and they see "anyone," only to be treated maliciously. A trans person may effectively retreat to protect themselves from a harmful provider, but in ways that increase social isolation, which is a suicide risk factor (Calati et al., 2019). Psychologists need to be alert to a trans client's experiences so that they can accurately recognize additional risks to the client's safety.

2.7.3 Nonsuicidal Self-Injury

Nonsuicidal self-injury (NSSI) is equally as common in trans people as depression is, by self-report (dickey et al., 2015). It would appear that, like cisgender people, most trans people will age out of this behavior. NSSI typically starts in adolescence, and many trans people will stop this behavior in early adulthood. It is unclear how a person's transition impacts their continued use of NSSI as a means of managing their emotional distress. Trans people may also use NSSI in a way that is different from their cisgender peers. This might include a move toward safety and health.

There are inter- and intrapersonal reasons for a person to engage in NSSI

Like other concerns, therapists should support their clients in managing their NSSI rather than treating this automatically as a contraindication to transition. Psychologists who are skilled in working with trans clients will be able to help them develop and implement prosocial coping skills. In the subsection on Dialectical Behavior Therapy (in Section 4.2.2: Therapeutic Approaches), we explore the use of *dialectical behavior therapy* (DBT) as an approach to working with trans clients. Given the ways that DBT has been shown to be effective with self-injury, we believe it will be useful for trans clients as well.

2.7.4 Reasonably Well-Controlled Mental Health

The WPATH SOC suggest that any mental health concerns be "reasonably well-controlled" prior to medical gender affirmation. The first author of this present work has defined "reasonably well-controlled" as (a) having an absence of symptoms or having only symptoms that do not interfere with functioning, (b) adhering to a medication treatment regimen, (c) having the ability to manage activities of daily living (e.g., personal hygiene, clothing oneself, meal preparation), (d) having the ability to self-regulate emotional changes, and/or (e) not being in imminent danger (e.g., active suicidal behavior without the ability to commit to a safety plan).

The SOC lack a definition of what it means to have mental health concerns reasonably well-controlled

It is common for trans people to experience one or more co-occurring mental health concerns. Even though that is the case, the symptoms of the disorder(s) may not be interfering with the client's life to such a significant degree that they would impede access to care. Technically, if most conditions do not cause significant distress or impairment that means that the disorder is not diagnosable.

Some mental health concerns are treated with medication(s). If the client is compliant with medications, they may not be experiencing symptoms that interfere with their life. As psychologists, few of us are trained to manage medications. Having contact with the medical provider who is prescribing and managing the client's medications will help to ensure that the treatment is addressing the client's symptoms. For instance, the first author worked in an integrated primary care clinic. This allowed him to collaborate with the medical providers who were also treating his patients. Because he saw the patients more often than the medical providers, he was able to work with the provider(s) when the medications were not working as intended.

A condition that is reasonably well-controlled is not likely to interfere with the client managing activities of daily living (ADLs). ADLs include activities in various aspects of a person's life such as the ability to manage personal hygiene, preparing or accessing food and other daily sustenance, and carrying out work or school activities. Another aspect to consider is whether a person has the ability to manage emotional changes. Sometimes, the emotional changes can be very difficult. Mental health providers play several roles in a client's life, and helping clients to obtain and effectively use coping skills can change their ability to regulate and cope with their emotions.

> **Clients may need support in managing NSSI or suicidality**

A final area to consider is whether the client is in imminent danger, such as endorsing high risk for suicidality without a commitment to a safety plan or other measures to protect the client. To be clear, as we outlined before, suicidality in and of itself should not automatically lead to the prevention of a person moving forward in their transition. This is more nuanced than a cut and dry rule, as we described in Section 2.7.2: Suicide and Trans People.

> **Strive to create a space that is the least difficult or restrictive for clients**

Psychologists are encouraged to find ways to support their trans clients in an effort to minimize disruption to the transition process. However, if a trans person is unwilling or unable to make and adhere to a safety plan, safety measures can and should be put in place to keep the client as safe as possible. If they cannot, then this can be an indication that their mental health concerns are not "reasonably well-controlled" at the time.

It is unlikely that all of these clinical concerns will apply to a given client. To the extent that they do, it will be important to be clear with the client what needs to happen for their symptoms to be reasonably well-controlled. For example, a client may be experiencing thoughts of ending their life. Helping the client to develop coping skills may be all that is needed to address thoughts of suicide. This is not meant to oversimplify suicidal ideation, which is a serious clinical concern. It does not, however, need to be a reason to deny access to care if the client is not in imminent risk and is able to engage in care and safety planning or other interventions. Hormone treatment has been shown to improve well-being for trans people (Keo-Meier et al., 2015). Even though the initiation of hormones can be difficult as a person becomes accustomed to the effects of the treatment, just being able to move forward can be enough to mitigate the intensity of suicidal thoughts. Ultimately, suicidality exists along a continuum and a thorough risk assessment is needed to determine what level of risk a given client is at. One person may need more immediate intervention such as hospitalization if they are not able to commit to a safety plan, have active thoughts and a plan they intend on carrying out with access to the means to do so. Another person may have passive ideation that comes and goes without a plan or intent. As such, simply endorsing suicidality should not be a reason to deny supports for medical affirmation – particularly given how common this is for trans people and that minority stress and gender dysphoria are triggers for suicidal ideation.

If you are working with a client whose mental health is compromised to the point that you do not feel confident in their ability to manage a transition, the client should have a clear understanding of what is expected for them to be ready to move forward. For example, they should be able to manage basic hygiene (e.g., ability to shower) and manage their medications. We are reluctant to hold to hard and fast descriptions of what reasonably well-controlled means. The reason for this is that some mental health providers have held to rigid expectations of what a trans person must do (e.g., the real-life test being forced on trans people, thereby requiring them to engage in behavior that puts them at risk or in danger). Providers should benefit from having some realistic expectations of what represents an indication that the client is ready to move forward with a transition without creating new sources of distress. Being transparent about this also empowers clients to make changes in their lives that will be to the benefit of their mental health and well-being.

Defining reasonably well-controlled can assist in understanding when clients may need support

2.7.5 Regret

A common theme among family members, especially parents, is the concern that their loved one will regret the decision to transition. It is difficult in the US to calculate levels of regret. This is primarily due to the fact that medical care is offered under many organizations and practices and is generally decentralized. Unlike some countries in Europe, there is no consolidated access to medical care in the US. Fortunately, we can look at the prevalence and regret data from Amsterdam and Sweden.

Regret for having transitioned is an uncommon experience

Wiepjes and colleagues (2018) reviewed medical records in Amsterdam for people who sought medical care, for the purposes of understanding the prevalence and regret rates of trans people from 1975 to 2015. Over 40 years, 6,793 people visited the clinic in Amsterdam for the purpose of accessing care for a medical transition. It is important to know that in the Netherlands there is the expectation that a trans person will access hormones and surgery. Over time, the percentage of trans people accessing hormones dropped from 90% to 65%. Of those who initiated hormone treatment, 74.7% of trans women and 83.8% of trans men completed gender affirmation surgeries (top and/or bottom surgery). Of those who had bottom surgery, 0.6% ($n = 41$) of trans women and 0.3% ($n = 20$) of trans men later expressed regret. Regret was defined as either being social or true. Social regret was related to the loss of family members or friends. True regret was explained as having believed that transition would change things such as having a sexual minority identity or self-acceptance. It is not clear how many of the people who had regret did anything to change their transition status.

The number of people who expressed regret in Sweden was higher than it was in Amsterdam. Approximately 2% of people who accessed care in Sweden later expressed regret. Dhejne and colleagues (2014) report that trans men who expressed regret did so at a median of 7.5 years after transition, and for trans women the median was 8.5 years after transition. Of note, current laws in Sweden require a person to be at least 18 years old and be a Swedish resident. This is a major shift from previous expectations that also required a trans person to be unmarried and sterile (e.g., have had a hysterectomy or

The process for accessing care outside of the United States may look very different

oophorectomy). To be able to access care in Sweden, a trans person is expected to have completed 12 months of evaluation. Then, after a minimum of 2 years during which a trans person will initiate hormone treatment, and have chest surgery in the case of trans masculine people or have engaged in hair removal and speech therapy in the case of trans feminine people. This happens while a trans individual is also completing a real-life experience (note that the real-life experience has not been a requirement of the SOC since 2012, which admittedly was enacted after the data collection period for Dhejne and colleagues [2014]).

In the Netherlands and Sweden, trans people who are experiencing regret can apply for a reversal of hormone and surgical treatment. The process of reversing the effects of transition is also known as *detransition.*

People who experience regret about transitioning may choose to reverse the effects of transition

It is unclear what the steps are for a person to reverse their transition in Sweden, only that they must apply to do so. Regret is uncommon, but not completely absent from some trans people's experiences. It is also unclear from the available literature why a person might choose to detransition based on regret. Is the regret based on the inability to transition in a way that allows the person to pass? (The term "pass" or "passing" is complicated. A person who is able to pass is not seen by others as having a trans history. Some trans people will not be able to pass. The reasons for this are varied, and foremost is the inability to access care from well-trained providers. Within the trans community, the term "passing" is fraught with difficulty because of the differences between how a person is or is not able to pass and many people dislike the term.) Is the regret based on the changes in relationships with friends and loved ones? Is the regret due to having lost their job and/or home? As one can see, regret can be due to any of the social determinants of health (SDOH). The fact that some people may experience regret speaks to the need to ensure that your clients have realistic expectations about what can, and what will not, happen as a part of transition. We also find it important to note that hyperfocusing on the possibility of regret can lead to fear mongering and microaggressions. Given the low percentages of people who endorse this, it is unlikely but providers should follow their clients' leads in terms of how much a concern this is for the person.

3

Assessment and Treatment Indications

Intakes with new clients generally include an assessment of their presenting concerns, learning about identity-related experiences, and understanding the contextual factors that influence a client's day-to-day life. Generally speaking, evidence-based practice should be followed in the assessment and treatment planning process, but we recognize that few such resources exist that were designed for trans people. Given that there has been minimal research about the effectiveness and validity of various assessment tools with trans clients, psychologists should be aware of this and how it may influence their interpretations of a client's responses. In this section, we detail various screening and assessment tools, as well as progress-monitoring tools that may be useful with trans clients, and concerns that may arise.

3.1 Assessment

One aspect of a psychologist's work portfolio is the ability to administer, score, and interpret psychological assessments. Although screening tools are often used by professionals with less training, the most complex personality and cognitive assessments are employed by psychologists or under the direction of a psychologist. We will devote considerable time here to the understanding of the various measures that have been developed for use with trans clients.

> Assessment is the work activity that distinguishes psychologists from other mental health providers

3.1.1 Screening Tools

Screening tools are used in clinical practice, as they have the ability to paint a picture of what is happening in the client's life. Screening tools and other measures should not be the only source of information, as they do not replace the knowledge that can be obtained with a quality intake interview and do not provide sufficient information to make a diagnosis. As such, they are only part of the data gathering and not the sole source of information.

Sheldrick and colleagues (2015) describe the required aspects of an effective screening tool. They start with the concept of *sensitivity* which refers to the screening tool being able to accurately predict the clinical concern. Next, they address *specificity,* which relates to the number of people who receive a negative result, where the clinical concern is not present. Finally, they refer to *positive* and *negative predictive values.* These values relate to the proportion of people who correctly receive a positive or negative result (Sheldrick et al.,

2015). One of the challenges that psychologists should be most concerned about is whether a screening tool, or any other type of assessment, has been normed with trans people. Unless an assessment measure was designed to be used specifically by trans clients, then the results should be interpreted with caution (we will address such measures in Section 3.1.5: Measures Designed for Trans Clients).

Examples of screening tools include the Beck Depression Inventory–II (BDI-II; Beck et al., 1996), the Beck Hopelessness Scale (BHS; Beck, 1993), the Depression, Anxiety and Stress Scale – 21 (DASS-21; Lovibond & Lovibond, 1995), the Patient Health Questionnaire-9 (PHQ-9; Kroenke et al., 2001), the Generalized Anxiety Disorder–7 (GAD-7; Spitzer et al., 2006), and the Adverse Childhood Experiences (ACE) survey (Felitti et al., 1998). Some of these tools can be used at no cost; others need to be purchased from a publisher. It can be easy for providers to focus on the answers to a specific question without understanding how other answers may paint a clearer picture of the client's symptoms. For example, the PHQ-9 has a question that asks, "do you have thoughts that you would be better off dead or of hurting yourself" (Kroenke et al., 2001, p. 613). Certainly, it is critical to understand if a person is at risk of hurting themselves, but it is also important to focus on a person's appetite and sleeping behaviors. In the end, screening tools are helpful for understanding basic clinical concerns and providers should follow up appropriately with a risk assessment if critical items about suicidality are endorsed while also attending to the full person's experiences. However, screening tools should never replace a thorough clinical interview leading to a diagnosis.

To date, screening measures such as those listed above are not normed for use with trans people. It is possible that a trans person may have participated in the studies related to the development of these measures. Because of the violence, discrimination, and mistreatment that many trans people experience, it is possible that the results of screening measures may be artificially elevated in ways that elicit clinical concern. It is useful to talk with the client about the reasons and experiences that are behind the elevated screening results. Psychologists need to be prepared to ask their trans clients about a history of substance abuse, suicidal thoughts or behavior, and trauma.

3.1.2 Outcome Measures

Outcome measures are useful in determining whether our services are effective in addressing the client's concerns. Just like screening measures, most outcome measures were normed using a general population. If there was a more specific group of people who were used to determine the validity and reliability of the tool, it is likely that they were a specific clinical group or an inpatient population.

It is important to use outcome measures in a way that allows you to gain an understanding of the effectiveness of your work with trans clients. Given the numerous ways that a trans client's experience can be invalidated both within and outside of therapy, it is important to know if there are ways that you have engaged in this type of communication. Nadal (2013) and Morris and colleagues (2020) explore the ways that *microaggressions* (everyday slights) can have the cumulative effect of being disrespectful at best and traumatic at worst. Given this, outcome measures that reflect treatment progress and the quality of the clinical relationship and alliance may be useful.

3.1.3 Critique of Personality Assessment Tools

Personality assessment tools such as the MMPI-2 (the MMPI-3 was recently published), the Personality Assessment Inventory (PAI), the Millon Clinical Multiaxial Inventory–IV (MCMI-IV), or the 16 Personality Factors (16PF) are often used in clinical practice for the purpose of determining the clinical concern a client is experiencing. Like screening tools, personality assessments have not been normed for use with trans people. The challenge for psychologists is how to select an assessment tool that will lead to accurate results for their trans clients, without pathologizing their lived experience.

One concern a psychologist must attend to is how to assign a gender (or sex) to clients which may be required for scoring purposes with some assessments. For example, if you have a client who was AFAB who has been living as a trans masculine person, how would you assign their gender? In justifying the assignment of female, there is the reality that the trans masculine person may have been primarily socialized as a female. However, some trans people know from a young age (as young as the age of 3) that their gender is different from the sex they were assigned at birth. Is using female norms appropriate for this client? Or should the instrument be scored for a male client?

Keo-Meier and Fitzgerald (2017) provided a landmark critical review of neurocognitive and personality assessment. Keo-Meier and Fitzgerald begin by describing the need for more than basic training in psychosocial assessment. Without this, the psychologist may make an inaccurate decision about the clinical needs of the client. Should this happen, the harm incurred by a trans person may be significant. Given the history of the use of personality assessments in making a determination of a client's readiness to transition, psychologists must be thoughtful about the selection and use of assessments.

> **Advanced training in the use of assessments is required**

Keo-Meier and Fitzgerald (2017) discuss the need for psychologists to have training and competency in the use of the *gender affirmative model* (GAM), the gender minority stress model, the ways that hormones may impact the client's mood, and how to score assessments for trans clients (as mentioned above).

The GAM is a conceptual approach to working with trans people. It starts with the belief that having a trans identity is not a disorder. This can be a difficult concept for a psychologist to accept, depending on their training. When psychologists assume there is something wrong with their patient, they may have trouble accepting the positive attributes of their clients. The GAM expects an understanding of the ways intersecting identities influence a person's gender experience (see Section 4.5.1: Intersectionality). Finally, psychologists understand the fluidity of gender and sexuality and that the source of pathology may have much more to do with discriminatory experiences than it does the person's gender.

> **The gender affirmative model is a conceptual framework for understanding the needs of trans people**

Keo-Meier and Fitzgerald (2017) spend considerable time critiquing the use of the MMPI-2. They begin by addressing the ways the assessment has been used and, in some cases, misused. They clearly explain the ways that trans people may be likely to have elevated scores that indicate clinically significant mental health concerns. They explore each of the clinical scales and provide clear advice about how to interpret elevated scores. For example, if a person has a clinically significant score on the depression and anxiety scales, they may not be anxious or depressed. Rather, they may be dealing with discrimination, minority stress, and other life concerns such as health disparities. Keo-Meier and Fitzgerald discuss the need to interpret the results with caution. One should not automatically assume pathology in trans clients. Even when the client presents with clinical concerns, there may be a number of reasons these concerns may not be the appropriate focus, as we discuss throughout this volume.

There may be a valid purpose for conducting assessments with trans clients. When the need arises, psychologists must be cautious in all aspects of assessment administration. This includes the clinical question(s) to be answered, the selection and administration of the assessment(s), and the scoring and interpretation. Of note, as of this writing, there are no affirmative assessments that could be used for the purpose of determining whether or not a person has a trans identity – we know this information about a person because of their endorsement of this identity, not because of assessment results.

3.1.4 Progress-Monitoring Tools

The types of progress-monitoring tools used for trans clients who are seeking mental health services should be aligned with the presenting problems of the client (e.g., depression symptoms) and should also be gender affirming and inclusive of trans people's experiences. For instance, some scales may contain items that include language of "he or she" and are not inclusive of people who use other pronouns. When clients are asked to fill out questionnaires like this or forms that ask about gender in a binary manner or which conflate sex and gender, the client's experience is invalidated. Sometimes forms that include sex or gender questions will have a blank to complete that is labeled "other" with a choice to write in a response. Although the logic around using that as a means for collecting data seems appropriate, the use of "other" can be *othering* to a trans person and can produce a rupture in the therapeutic relationship. It also likely impacts the validity of these scales.

"Othering" a person is dehumanizing

3.1.5 Measures Designed for Trans Clients

Limited measures have been developed specifically for trans people, and many of the existing mental health measures were validated with cisgender samples (see Shulman et al., 2017, for a review of measures available; Table 3 has a list of measures that have been developed for trans people or work with trans people). As such, there may be limited options for providers seeking progress monitoring or outcome measures to include in their work with trans clients. The measures that have been developed with trans clients may help to assess mechanisms or treatment targets, such as internalized stigma via the Gender Minority Stress and Resilience Scale (Testa et al., 2015). Another scale is the Trans Collaborations Clinical Check-In (TC^3; Holt et al., 2019) that was developed using community-based research methods and has been validated as

Table 3
List of assessment tools that were developed for trans people

Assessment	Source
Gender Congruence and Life Satisfaction Scale (GCLS)	Jones, B. A., Bouman, W. P., Haycraft, E., & Arcelus, J. (2019). The Gender Congruence and Life Satisfaction Scale (GCLS): Development and validation of a scale to measure outcomes from transgender health services. *International Journal of Transgenderism. 20*(1), 63–80. https://doi.org/10.1080/15532739.2018.1453425
Gender Embodiment Scale: Trans Masculine Spectrum	DuBois, L. Z., Puckett, J. A., & Langer, S. J. (2021). Development of the Gender Embodiment Scale: Trans Masculine Spectrum. *Transgender Health*. Advance online publication. https://doi.org/10.1089/trgh.2020.0088
Gender Identity Reflection and Rumination Scale (GRRS)	Bauerband, L. A., & Galupo, M. P. (2014). The gender identity reflection and rumination scale: Development and psychometric evaluation. *Journal of Counseling & Development, 92*, 219–231. https://doi.org/10.1002/j.1556-6676.2014.001251.x
Gender Minority Stress and Resilience Scale (GMSRS)	Testa, R. J., Habarth, J., Peta, J., Balsam, K., & Bockting, W. (2015). Development of the Gender Minority Stress and Resilience Measure. *Psychology of Sexual Orientation and Gender Diversity, 2*(1), 65–77. https://doi.org/10.1037/sgd0000081
Strength of Transgender Identity Scale (STIS)	Barr, S. M., Budge, S. L., & Adelson, J. L. (2016). Transgender community belongingness as a mediator between strength of transgender identity and well-being. *Journal of Counseling Psychology, 63*, 87–97. https://doi.org/10.1037/cou0000127
Transgender Adaptation and Integration Measure (TG AIM)	Sjoberg, M. D., Walch, S. E., & Stanny, C. J. (2006). Development and initial psychometric evaluation of the Transgender Adaptation and Integration Measure (TG AIM). *International Journal of Transgenderism, 9*(2), 35–45. https://doi.org/10.1300/J485v09n02_05
Transgender Community Belongingness (TCB)	Barr, S. M., Budge, S. L., & Adelson, J. L. (2016). Transgender community belongingness as a mediator between strength of transgender identity and well-being. *Journal of Counseling Psychology, 63*, 87–97. https://doi.org/10.1037/cou0000127
Transgender Congruence Scale (TCS)	Kozee, H. B., Tylka, T. L., & Bauerband, L. A. (2012). Measuring transgender individuals' comfort with gender identity and appearance: Development and validation of the Transgender Congruence Scale. *Psychology of Women Quarterly, 36*, 179–196. https://doi.org/10.1177/0361684312442161
Transgender Positive Identity Measure (T-PIM)	Riggle, E. B., & Mohr, J. J. (2015). A proposed multi factor measure of positive identity for transgender identified individuals. *Psychology of Sexual Orientation and Gender Diversity, 2*, 78–85. https://doi.org/10.1037/sgd0000082

Table 3. Continued

Assessment	Source
Transgender Voice Questionnaire for Male-to-Female Transsexuals (TVQ^{MTF})	Dacakis, G., Davies, S., Oates, J. M., Douglas, J. M., & Johnston, J. R. (2013). Development and preliminary evaluation of the Transsexual Voice Questionnaire for male-to-female transsexuals. *Journal of Voice, 27,* 312–320. https://doi.org/10.1037/t28993-000
Transgender-Related Intimate Partner Violence	Peitzmeier, S. M., Hughto, J. M. W., Potter, J., Deutsch, M. B., & Reisner, S. L. (2019). Development of a novel tool to assess intimate partner violence against transgender individuals. *Journal of Interpersonal Violence, 34*(11), 2376–2397. https://doi.org/10.1177/0886260519827660
Utrecht Gender Dysphoria Scale (UGDS)	Cohen-Kettenis, P. T., & van Goozen, S. H. M. (1997). Sex reassignment of adolescent transsexuals: A follow-up study. *Journal of the American Academy of Child and Adolescent Psychiatry, 36,* 263–271. https://doi.org/10.1097/00004 583-19970 2000-00017
Workplace Identity Management Scale – Transgender Form	Brewster, E. M., Velez, B. L., Deblaere, C., & Moradi, B. (2011). Transgender individuals' workplace experiences: The applicability of sexual minority measures and models. *Journal of Counseling Psychology, 59*(1), 60–70. https://doi.org/10.1037/a0025206

Based on Galupo & Pulice-Farrow, 2020, and Shulman et al., 2017.

a progress monitoring tool that assesses a variety of areas, including comfort with one's body, exposure to stigma, and social supports.

Another tool that may help trans masculine clients in exploring their gender is the Gender Embodiment Scale (DuBois et al., 2021). The Gender Embodiment Scale has a variety of questions that provide trans masculine clients with the opportunity to reflect on physical or behavioral ways of expressing a masculine gender experience, and it allows the client to rate both the importance of each item, as well as their satisfaction with these characteristics. Notably, this scale inherently incorporates a diverse understanding of gender and an acknowledgement that gender experiences can vary across individuals even within the same gender group. Through providing the opportunity for clients to indicate what aspects of their body or behavior are important to them, rather than assuming a one size fits all understanding of gender experiences, providers can become cognizant of the diverse experiences of gender that exist within the community. The Gender Embodiment Scale can also be used as a tool to facilitate a discussion with psychologists about steps that clients may want to take to affirm their gender.

Assessment tools can be useful for tracking therapy progress and learning more about clients' experiences. It is important that providers maintain critical mindfulness of what population each measure was created for, validated with, and the implications of this for accurate representation of trans individuals' lived experiences. Taking a strengths-based approach, providers should also

> The Gender Embodiment Scale is one of a growing set of resources that are designed for trans people

consider measures of support and resources and not just symptomatology. This will help providers to learn more about the ways that they can enhance positive outcomes for their clients.

In terms of positive experiences that psychologists may want to assess, this should be matched to what is most relevant to a given client. Some options include identity pride and community connectedness, which could be assessed using the GMSRS (Testa et al., 2015). Another option is to measure resilience more generally. Although there are no scales that were created to measure resilience for trans people in the broad sense of being able to bounce back from challenges, the Brief Resilience Scale (Smith et al., 2008) has been used in several studies with trans participants, with high levels of reliability. Even so, there are unique forms of resilience for trans people that are often neglected in this type of measure, such as the development of critical consciousness and self-advocacy efforts. Overall, more measure development is needed, particularly for assessing strengths and resilience in the lives of trans people.

Measures of positive aspects of identity and resilience are severely underdeveloped for trans populations

3.1.6 Caution When Interpreting Results

The interpretation of a clinical assessment is often subjective and based on the clinical paradigms to which a psychologist ascribes. Any time an assessment is completed for a trans client, the assessment report should include the phraseology: "use caution when interpreting or implementing the results of this assessment." The logic behind this is due to the challenges associated with determining how to assign gender on an assessment for a trans client. It is also related to the types of challenges that trans people face on a day-to-day basis. Discriminatory and violent behavior that is aimed at trans people understandably will impact a person's overall well-being.

Always use caution when interpreting assessment results for trans clients

4

Treatment

Much more research is needed evaluating evidence-based interventions with trans clients

There has been minimal research about interventions that are effective with trans clients. Much of the existing literature has focused on case studies, summaries of treatment adaptations, and guidance based on clinical experience. Although this is helpful in providing guidance for clinicians and information that can help improve mental health services, there has been minimal empirical evaluation of interventions with trans clients. As such, there is much to be learned about the types of interventions that are effective in addressing the unique experiences that come up for trans clients, such as minority stressors, or about how to adapt treatments for presenting concerns such as depression or PTSD, to make them affirming for trans clients. Overall, there is a great need for research about both intervention development and treatment adaptation to improve the quality of care that trans clients receive.

4.1 Method of Treatment

Counseling is not a requirement for gender affirming medical care

Overall, psychologists must differentiate the method of treatment depending on the client's presenting concerns. An initial consult with a client should include exploring whether a client is seeking counseling or if they are seeking a letter of support for gender-affirming medical care. If the latter, counseling is *not* a requirement, and imposing this expectation on your client is harmful, as it hinders their access to gender-affirming medical care that has been shown to improve mental health and well-being (Keo-Meier et al., 2015).

If, on the other hand, a client is seeking counseling, or it would be useful due to a need to address mental health concerns that are not reasonably well-controlled, psychologists will need to make decisions about the best treatment approach for a given client. This should be based on the specific mental health concern of the client (e.g., depression, anxiety, obsessive-compulsive disorder, or PTSD) and psychologists should utilize evidence-based practices in shaping their treatment choices and approach. In this section, we review the available literature about the efficacy and prognosis of therapy and adaptations that will likely help psychologists to provide more affirming care with trans clients.

4.1.1 Specific Clinical Concerns

It is not uncommon for trans people to have co-occurring mental health concerns (APA, 2015). Reports of substance abuse, depression, anxiety, and

PTSD are not uncommon. Psychologists need to work with their clients to determine the treatment plan which addresses those concerns that the client finds most challenging and is prepared to address. We discuss these common clinical concerns and highlight the recent literature for each concern. It is possible that a trans person is coming to see you because they have questions about their gender, rather than seeking treatment for a specific mental health concern. Providers should provide space for clients to explore their gender. We also caution against rooting other mental health issues in a person's gender – this is pathologizing and stigmatizing. It is also possible, although infrequent, that a trans person will see you because mental health concerns that are mimicking gender concern (e.g., psychosis, dissociative identity; APA, 2015; Chang et al., 2018). Having the ability to understand the nuanced differences as you contemplate a differential diagnosis that will influence treatment planning is one of the reasons psychologists who work with trans people need more than basic training.

> It is unlikely that a trans person will have a serious mental illness that mimics gender identity

Substance Abuse

People often engage in substance use for the purpose of avoiding difficult experiences and feelings. One of the challenges we have with regard to research about trans people's substance use behaviors is that trans people are often included with lesbian, gay, and bisexual people. This means that we are not able to drill down to the substance use rates for trans people as easily as we may be for other populations.

> Many studies lump trans people together with cisgender LGB people

Research has shown that lesbian, gay, bisexual, and transgender (LGBT) adolescents are at greater risk for substance use than their cisgender, heterosexual peers (Huebner et al., 2015). Huebner and colleagues utilized a social development model to explore the underpinnings of substance use in LGBT adolescents. They assumed that experiences of harassment, discrimination, and victimization were reasons for substance use. One of the limitations of the study is that the inclusion criteria sought out only LGB adolescents, not trans participants specifically. This is consistent with the point made at the beginning of this section: It can be challenging to find accurate data because of the ways this type of research is conducted. Not surprisingly, the results of their study indicate that LGBT youths use drugs and alcohol at higher rates than their cisgender, heterosexual counterparts. Drug and alcohol use was attributed to the violence, discrimination, and harassment that LGBT youths frequently face. In a study of trans youths in the California public middle and high schools, researchers found that the substance abuse rates were higher for trans teens (De Pedro et al., 2017). Trans students were 2.5 times more likely to have used methamphetamine or cocaine, 2.8 times as likely to use an inhalant, twice as likely to report prescription pain medication, and 3 times as likely to use cigarettes in school (De Pedro et al., 2017).

Another study was devoted to understanding how trans adults were different from cisgender adults when entering substance abuse treatment (Flentje et al., 2014). Using a deidentified data set from San Francisco County, the authors were able to compare the experiences of trans and cisgender people based on intake interviews. Absent from the results are how people with non-binary identities differed from cisgender people. Trans men were more likely than cisgender men to have had a job in the past month, less likely to have had

> Trans men were less likely to have legal issues and more likely to be employed than cisgender men

involvement with the judicial system, more likely to live with a person who engages in substance use, and more likely to have encountered family conflict.

Trans women, on the other hand, were less likely to have minor children, and there were no other significant differences on any other demographic variables. Trans women and trans men were more likely to have experienced issues with their physical health. There was no significant difference in the age at which a person began using drugs or alcohol, there was also no difference in the primary substance of abuse, but trans women were more likely to use methamphetamine than cisgender women.

In a 3-year longitudinal study, Nuttbrock and colleagues (2014) explored gender abuse (which they define as enacted stigma), depression, and substance abuse. At baseline, 76.2% of participants reported any substance use. Gender abuse was associated with substance use including alcohol, cannabis, and cocaine. Depression was found to mediate the association of gender abuse and substance use. It is important to note that the findings from this study were for trans women (Nuttbrock et al., 2014).

Depression and Anxiety

Trans people have high rates of depression and anxiety, and these mood states are often explored together. Earlier we discussed the ways that minority stress influences trans people's lives, and this can include experiences of depression and anxiety (see Section 2.1: Minority Stress Theory). We should not forget to explore the kinds of challenges a person faces. Many trans people have few resources to aid their transition process. If they lose their job after coming out to their employer (which is illegal at a federal level but not in all states), a cascade of challenges may be ready to be released. Trans people are more likely to be unemployed, homeless, and are almost always included in "religious exemption laws" (Movement Advancement Project [MAP], 2021).

> Religious exemption laws typically include trans people

In a study of youths (Thorne et al., 2019), nonbinary adolescents had significantly higher rates of anxiety and depression and at the same time showed lower levels of self-esteem. Klemmer and colleagues (2018) explored the links between transphobia-based violence and depression and anxiety in trans women. Participants reported high rates of depression (57.5%) and anxiety (42.1%). Compared with the rates for the general population, these results are alarmingly high. According to the Centers for Disease Control and Prevention (Villarroel & Terlizzi, 2020), 18.5% of adults experienced mild to severe symptoms of depression within the previous 2-week window. Just over 11% of adults in the general population report symptoms of anxiety (T. C. Clarke et al., 2020). In an epidemiological review, Bazrafshan and colleagues (2021) report rates of depression in trans people to be between 40% and 60% and of anxiety to be between 26% and 44%. Again, these rates are much higher than what we see in the general population.

> Trans people experience alarmingly high rates of depression and anxiety

In a systematic review, Millet and colleagues (2016) found that 17–68% of trans people experienced some form of anxiety (e.g., specific phobia, panic disorder, social phobia, obsessive-compulsive disorder). Borgogna and colleagues (2018) had similar findings and also found that people who have emerging sexual and gender minority (SGM) identities (e.g., demisexual, pansexual, questioning, trans, and gender nonconforming) have even higher rates. They make several recommendations for clinical practice. They start with the need to be open and accepting to people who have an emerging SGM identity and to attend to the intersectionality that is part of many people's experience. They remind providers of the need to remain current with the latest information about SGM individuals and not to rely on their client to provide that information. Borgogna and colleagues also suggest the need to make interventions at the institutional level such as a *safe space* or *safe zone*.

Institutional interventions may be needed

If you are going to use stickers or decals from LGTBQ+ organizations, it is critical to ensure that you understand not only how to display these emblems, but also the ways that an organization may not be trans friendly, even if they include "T" in their name. There are two examples that help to clarify this point. The first author collected used cell phones from fellow students while attending graduate school. The purpose of collecting the phones was to donate them to a domestic violence shelter. As he approached the door of the shelter, he saw a pink triangle very prominently displayed. Although the shelter was making a good effort to indicate that they were welcoming of LGBTQ+ residents, the shelter did not realize that the triangle was upside down. This sent a message to the first author that while the shelter was trying to be welcoming, they fell short as they did not know how to display the pink triangle. Imagine if a prospective shelter resident had finally mustered the courage to seek shelter, only to find that the only option in town was a shelter that did not really understand LGBTQ+ people and their needs. Second, caution should be used to ensure that you have an understanding of the complicated history some LGBTQ+ organizations have with trans communities. Not all organizations fully embrace the needs of trans people (dickey, 2016).

In reviewing the various co-occurring mental health concerns, it is clear that intersecting identities is not just about demographic factors, but it is also about the mental health concerns that a person is experiencing. There are many ways that trans people experience health challenges. Challenges can also arise from the need to delay care. This might happen because a person is not able to afford care, they do not have access to affirming providers, or they lack health insurance (which is related to affordability). Providing access to care requires more than simply opening up an office. Even though most psychologists should have sufficient skills to provide care for their clients, without having made an effort to understand the unique challenges trans people face and the ways those needs influence their safety, more training or supervision may be necessary.

The presence of other mental health concerns could be considered an intersecting identity

4.2 Efficacy and Prognosis

Research shows that trans individuals face many challenges when seeking mental health services, ranging from providers holding outdated understandings of gender, to being openly hostile and stigmatizing of trans individuals (Puckett et al., 2018). In addition, it is not uncommon for trans people to report having to educate their providers about gender and about being trans (Baldwin et al., 2018; James et al., 2016). Approximately one out of four trans people report that they had to educate their health care provider about trans experiences, over the past year (James et al., 2016). Furthermore, providers

There is no excuse for the ways that trans people are often treated with subpar approaches

themselves report being undertrained and lacking skills in working with trans clients (APA, 2015). We know that trans clients are receiving subpar therapy services from many providers and that much can be done to improve the services of providers.

Research related to treatment has typically examined the challenges that show up for trans clients, rather than an empirical evaluation of therapy services that may be (more) affirming, and this area of research is still in its infancy. For instance, research has shown that providers engage in a variety of gatekeeping practices that result in clients being stigmatized and feeling that their providers are questioning the legitimacy of their gender identities (Puckett et al., 2018). Trans clients also report a variety of microaggressions on the part of psychologists, such as misgendering clients, using pejorative terms to refer to clients, being dismissive of clients' identities, and fetishizing clients' experiences and identities (Morris et al., 2020). Other forms of microaggressions may include overemphasizing or underemphasizing a client's gender identity as hyper focusing on this area may feel marginalizing, as does ignoring this aspect of a person's experiences (Morris et al., 2020).

> **Both over and under emphasizing a client's gender can be problematic and stigmatizing**

As discussed in the following sections, there has been minimal research on the effectiveness of affirming interventions. As highlighted by Pachankis and Safren (2019), most research evaluating therapy interventions has focused more broadly on mental health conditions, such as depression or anxiety, and has failed to include affirming and inclusive measurement of gender. The lack of questions about gender has resulted in limited knowledge about the efficacy for such interventions with trans clients. Currently there is extremely limited knowledge about whether these interventions are effective, if they work in the same way, or if they need adaptations for trans clients. To date, much of what has been written about treatment with trans clients has been based on the assumption that entirely new treatments are likely not needed but that adaptations to care are imperative to making treatment effective and affirming. For instance, instead of creating a new treatment for depression experienced by trans clients, many researchers have written about the adaptations to cognitive behavioral interventions that would make the treatment theoretically more affirming and effective.

> **Existing approaches need to be adapted rather than creating new clinical approaches**

4.2.1 Affirmative Practice

Counter to stigmatizing actions on the part of providers, there are a variety of ways to engage in affirming practice – some of which have been reviewed in Sections 2.6 and 2.7. According to Anzani and colleagues (2019), trans clients report specific behaviors as affirming and resulting in positive experiences in therapy. At a base level, trans clients benefit when their psychologists do not engage in microaggressions, such as when they focus on a presenting problem rather than overemphasizing a person's gender as the problem. Trans clients also desire for psychologists to acknowledge cisnormativity, such as acknowledging binary language in their forms. Beyond this acknowledgement, psychologists who disrupt cisnormativity may further benefit their clients by providing the space for clients to explore and affirm their identities without any imposed understandings of gender. Finally, these positive qualities of psychologists and

> **Cisnormativity can happen in therapy, regardless of the provider's own gender identity**

services create an atmosphere in which clients feel affirmed and that psychologists recognize their authentic gender experiences.

In relation to specific clinical interventions that have been shown to be affirming of trans clients, much of what has been written is from a theoretical standpoint rather than an empirical evaluation of these intervention methods (Budge & Moradi, 2018; Pachankis, 2018). In 2017, Catelan and colleagues (2017) conducted a scoping review of research about psychological interventions with trans clients. They concluded that most of the research about interventions with this population was dated, with 48% of relevant studies having been published from 1980 to 1999. Furthermore, most of the studies were case studies or utilized small sample sizes – only 6% of the studies had samples larger than five participants. In addition, 78% were coded as describing reparative therapy practices, leaving much unknown about affirming practices with trans clients. In 2018, Budge and Moradi attempted to conduct a meta-analysis of randomized clinical trials (RCTs) evaluating therapy services with trans clients but were not able to find *any* articles that met their inclusion criteria. One of the reasons for this lack of research is that gender identity is often measured in problematic ways in demographics questions in treatment research (Pachankis, 2018), leaving questions about who is included in treatment evaluation studies and how treatment responses may differ across subgroups.

> A 2018 meta-analysis failed to find a single RCT conducted with trans participants

Recently, some empirical evaluation of therapy interventions with trans clients has been conducted. Budge and colleagues (2021) conducted an RCT comparing therapy that was described as being trans affirming, with therapy that met these same basics of being trans affirming but also incorporated interventions around building awareness of minority stressors. Clients in the latter treatment group tended to be more likely to engage in a higher number of sessions, showed declines in nonaffirmation and internalized stigma, and maintained positive outcomes (decreases in OQ-45 scores) at the 6-month follow-up, compared with the only trans-affirming condition. Both treatments were viewed positively by clients, had strong working alliances, and positive outcomes were reported for clients in both conditions. Although these trends were present in the data, many of the analyses were not statistically significant given the small sample size. Future RCTs with a larger sample are needed.

> A challenge for researchers working with trans people is the difficulty of finding a sufficient sample

In an evaluation of college counseling center data, Lefevor and colleagues (2019) found that trans clients had more severe symptoms than cisgender clients. Trans clients also attended more therapy sessions than cisgender clients and showed a slower decline in their symptoms. Although it is difficult to know the reason for this, it could be that higher levels of symptom severity was the reason for a slower decline and the greater number of sessions attended for trans clients. It also may be that therapy services do not adequately address the concerns of trans clients, resulting in these differing response rates. Similarly, trans youths have been shown to have higher levels of symptoms at the start of treatment compared with cisgender youths and slower responses to treatment (Hollinsaid et al., 2020).

Overall, more empirical research is needed that evaluates therapy interventions and adaptations for therapy with trans clients. At this stage in the literature, there has been very little investigation, and there is a clear need for more research in this area.

> More research is needed to build our knowledge of evidence-based practice with trans clients

4.2.2 Therapeutic Approaches

Some existing theoretical approaches easily lend themselves to trans-affirmative care

Given that much of the writing on clinical practice with trans clients has been theoretical or reflective in nature instead of empirical evaluations of these methods, we review these types of contributions here as well. Drawing from these theoretical writings, a few points are consistently viewed as essential for affirming practices. For one, providers should be sure to integrate an understanding of contextual factors and aspects of socialization, intersectionality, and marginalization, to better understand a client's lived experiences and presenting problem (Austin et al., 2016; Pachankis, 2018). When providers integrate this information into their case conceptualizations, they will have a more accurate and helpful understanding of their clients' lives and what may be helpful from an intervention standpoint (Matsuno, 2019). Developing case conceptualizations that integrate social systems will help psychologists to avoid pathologizing their clients or their responses to systemic oppression which may be normative and expected (Budge & Moradi, 2018).

Cognitive Behavior Therapy

Integrating contextual factors into CBT helps validate clients' lived experiences

Through a *cognitive behavior therapy* (CBT) lens, experiences of oppression may shape the types of automatic thoughts or underlying core beliefs that drive or are associated with a variety of presenting problems. A client who has experienced a high degree of social stigma associated with their trans identity may believe that they are a person of low worth or are inherently flawed, which may manifest as social isolation and broader negative self-judgments. Being sure to integrate these basic understandings of how socialization and marginalization have shaped clients' experiences enhances the case conceptualization and helps ensure that psychologists are validating the real challenges that have shaped their clients' life experiences (Matsuno, 2019).

Most of the literature addressing the use of CBT with trans clients also focuses on other clinical concerns (e.g., depression, suicidality). Austin and colleagues (2016) make the case for the use of transgender-affirmative CBT (TA-CBT). This approach to treatment recognizes the importance of having an affirmative approach with trans clients, considering the many stressors that trans people face (James et al., 2016), and approaching work from a trauma-informed stance (Austin et al., 2016).

Dialectical Behavior Therapy

The focus in DBT on the invalidating environment can be easily translated to work with trans clients

Another approach that may be easily modified to address the experiences of trans individuals is *dialectical behavior therapy* (DBT). This approach emphasizes that mental health issues arise as a product of the interactions between an invalidating environment and the person (including their temperament and any vulnerability factors – known as the biosocial model; Sloan & Berke, 2018). This theory fits with understanding the experiences of many trans clients, due to the importance of context and environment in understanding the development of emotion dysregulation.

As recognized by MST, there are many ways in which the identities and experiences of trans clients are invalidated – whether that be via overt forms of enacted stigma, rejection from one's family and peers, or being exposed to negative political rhetoric that portrays trans people in pathological ways. As a product of this chronic invalidation, trans individuals may develop issues with emotion regulation or other psychological processes. This is an understandable reaction to systemic oppression. DBT can be used to help clients learn to regulate their emotions, respond effectively in times of marginalization, and improve their distress tolerance when this is needed.

DBT has been useful as an approach to helping clients manage their distress and learn how to engage in prosocial relationships. Social isolation can be a significant source of emotional pain and has been linked to suicide risk (Calati et al., 2019). When trans clients are equipped with skills that help them manage the rough spots, they are more likely to be engaged with others. Having strong coping skills helps a client to address and manage the times when they are feeling stuck.

The myriad skills that are part of a DBT approach can be very helpful for trans people

Power Dynamics

Providers need to attend to power dynamics in the room when working with trans clients (Budge & Moradi, 2018). Psychologists hold a great amount of power over their clients, especially trans clients who are seeking an evaluation or a letter of support related to medical gender affirmation. These power dynamics should be explicitly named and discussed with clients. Psychologists are encouraged to use approaches that empower their clients (Matsuno, 2019) and to explore ways of using their privileges as psychologists to engage in advocacy for their clients (Pachankis, 2018; Sloan & Shipherd, 2019). It simply is not sufficient to help clients to cope with and endure marginalization. Psychologists must take an additional step to engage in changing these systems to further benefit their clients and trans individuals more broadly. Puckett (2019) provides an overview of a variety of strategies psychologists can use to engage in micro, mezzo, and macro level changes and to reduce cissexism. We provide a brief summary of the strategies in Table 4.

Psychologists must be mindful of the power they have in their work with trans clients

Table 4
Ecological framework for practice suggestions

Level	Suggestion
Macro	• Inform policy and practice through presentations • Be a consultant • Disrupt oppression of trans people • Advocate for legislative changes that are trans affirming
Mezzo	• Address barriers that impact access to care • Ensure confidentiality and minimize invasion of privacy • Provide a range of services that meet the varied needs of trans clients • Train everyone in your practice to be trans affirming • In inpatient settings ensure that visitation policies are trans inclusive
Micro	• Acknowledge the complicated history of psychology and trans people • Be transparent about your policies (including letter writing) • Create an affirming space • When mistakes happen, acknowledge them and move on

Adapted from Puckett, 2019.

Power is closely tied to the practice of gatekeeping. Specifically, when any client is relying on the support of a mental health provider to gain access to medical treatment, the provider has all of the power. Sadly, as noted in Section 1.4: Gatekeeping, gatekeeping has been used in very harmful ways in the past. To say that gatekeeping is no longer a problem would be patently false. Not unlike the ways that conversion therapy is harmful, so too are abuses of power that take advantage of the client's situation.

Integrating Minority Stress Theory
Given the empirical literature showing that trans individuals encounter high rates of minority stress, it is important that psychologists be thoughtful about how to integrate MST into practice. This information is meant to assist psychologists in making the modifications to their care that can help their interventions be more affirming and better able to attend to the unique experiences of trans clients. Because the specific interventions that a psychologist implements may vary across theoretical orientation (e.g., cognitive behavioral, interpersonal), we have provided some general recommendations that could be used regardless of orientation and in keeping with the MST framework.

> Framing your work with an eye toward MST will help to address common sources of stress

At the core of this suggestion is the seemingly simple principle that trans clients' experiences (really, all clients' experiences) should be understood within their context. This means that psychologists need to ask questions that allow for an understanding of individual symptoms of mental health issues to be understood within the context of clients' lives. For instance, if a client presents as socially anxious, withdrawn, and isolated, but a psychologist does not acknowledge their trans identity, the fact that their family disowned them after coming out, and their experience 2 years ago of a hate crime, this psychologist will be missing major life stressors that would be essential for a strong conceptualization leading to effective interventions. If a psychologist has minimized the importance of a client's identity, they could risk invalidating this client and having a rupture in the relationship (e.g., if a psychologist is dismissive or expresses confusion about why the client feels distrustful of others).

> Understanding the context in which a person lives and works is essential

To aid in developing this type of case conceptualization, psychologists can explore issues of marginalization and identity-related experiences as part of their standard intake procedures. This will allow psychologists to have a broad understanding of what the client has experienced and provide an opening for discussions about how this past relates to the client's current presenting concerns. We have provided a case formulation worksheet inspired by the work of Berke and Sloan (2019; see Appendix 1) that psychologists can use to help them make connections between the client's experiences. This form includes a section to detail the distal and proximal stressors that trans clients may report (see Section 2.1: Minority Stress Theory). It also provides a space to take note of the social narratives that the client expresses having been impacted by (e.g., internalized beliefs that they will never be happy as a trans person; anticipated experiences of discrimination, violence, and mistreatment). Psychologists can also take note of environmental or contextual factors that they should keep in mind (e.g., if living in a locale with antitrans legislation being proposed or enacted). Finally, the relational context of the

> Social connections are very important for trans people

client's interactions with family, friends, and others will provide important details to support the conceptualization.

Psychologists who emphasize a client's gender or experiences of marginalization too strongly will risk damaging their relationship with clients, and this should be avoided. Some clients will find a singular focus on their gender to be stigmatizing. There are no hard and fast rules as to when focusing on a particular aspect of a client's lived experience falls into a problematic area. Instead, psychologists should approach this work of integrating minority stress with openness to feedback and transparency. For instance, psychologists can make statements like "Sometimes people may feel anxious after they've experienced social rejection from others based on their gender. Is this something that has happened for you? If so, do you see any connections between that and your current experiences?" Psychologists can also pose hypotheses to their clients about connections to previous experiences and ask clients if this is consistent with their life or if they view it differently. This is a time where it is essential that psychologists remain humble. Although we have expertise about many things, our clients are the experts on their own lives and experiences, and their understanding of how presenting problems do and do not relate to their gender experiences should be respected.

> **Clients are experts of their own lives**

Resilience

Psychologists should consider integrating a resilience approach to their work with trans clients, including focusing on their unique strengths (Matsuno & Israel, 2018). To do so, providers should consider group-level resilience factors (e.g., community belongingness, social support, activism) and individuals' resilience factors (e.g., hope, self-worth, gender affirmation) that may promote positive outcomes for their clients (Matsuno & Israel, 2018). Promoting resilience may also include helping clients find connections with other trans individuals, building community connections, and developing a sense of pride in their gender identity to counter messages of shame (Matsuno & Israel, 2018; Pachankis, 2018).

> **Generally stated, resilience is the ability a person has to bounce back from a difficult experience**

One factor that has been shown to be important for developing resilience is *critical consciousness* (Freire, 1970), or the understanding that one's experience is embedded within social systems that marginalize minority groups. Without critical consciousness, clients may blame themselves for negative experiences, have low self-worth, or view their lives as less valuable than those of cisgender people. Developing critical consciousness as a resilience factor can empower trans clients to externalize blame when appropriate. For instance, a client may make statements about how they are "causing" their family to be upset and "harming" their partner by coming out. These types of statements are often indicative of internalized stigma, as trans people learn to view themselves as a source of problems due to the social narratives to which they are exposed. In this situation, a psychologist can help clients to question their beliefs and where they come from, ultimately leading to higher levels of critical consciousness.

> **Critical consciousness helps clients recognize the broader social system that oppresses trans people**

Developing agency and the ability to self-define a client's own gender experience is an important aspect that can lead to the promotion of resilience (Singh et al., 2011, 2014). Often, clients have been subjected to having their gender experience interrogated by others, questioned, belittled, or invalidated.

> **Trans people may internalize the negative messages they have heard from others**

As a result, clients may learn to adhere to stereotypes of gender experiences or may hesitate about coming out or affirming their gender. Psychologists can work with clients to explore their views of their gender experience and options for affirming their gender (e.g., social, legal, or medical forms of transition) to help clients deepen their understandings of their gender and develop agency.

Social support and connection with other trans people are an essential part of many trans individual's journeys to developing positive views of themselves. There are many negative messages that trans people are subjected to about the quality of life that trans people will have or about how they will lose support from others in their life. Due to this, trans people rarely hear positive experiences or messages about the strength and resilience of other trans people. Psychologists can help their clients to become more connected to social groups or support networks with other trans people to diversify the messages that they receive about trans people. This type of work may also entail exploring barriers to connecting with others, social skills development, or fears about others knowing that the client is trans. There exist numerous books that explore trans people's lives from a biographical perspective. You will find a list of titles and authors in Appendix 4 and Appendix 5.

> **There may be a need for our clients to hear about the success stories of trans people**

Medical Gender Affirmation

When it comes to evaluations for gender-affirming medical care, there are issues that clients may face with providers who do not support and in fact hinder their pursuit of hormones or surgery to affirm their gender (Morris et al., 2020; Puckett et al., 2018). There has been a movement for hormones to be provided using an informed consent framework, as this respects trans individuals' autonomy, decision making, and knowledge of their own experiences (Ashley, 2021; shuster, 2019).

Overall, research shows that medically affirming one's gender, for individuals who desire to pursue this form of affirmation, is associated with positive outcomes. A systematic review of hormone treatment in trans individuals younger than 25 years concluded that the use of puberty blockers was associated with improved mental health outcomes, although they did not find improvements in gender dysphoria, and more research is needed in this area (Chew et al., 2018). Other research has shown that use of hormone therapy, specifically testosterone, is associated with improvements in psychological functioning according to scores on the MMPI-2 at 3 months after initiation of treatment (Keo-Meier et al., 2015). In addition, a recent systematic review concluded that hormone therapy was associated with improvements in mental health for trans individuals and may be specifically associated with improved quality of life for trans women (White Hughto & Reisner, 2016).

> **In general, research supports that medical gender affirmation is associated with positive psychosocial outcomes**

In terms of surgical gender affirmation, research in Sweden has shown that trans individuals are less likely to engage in mental health treatment as more time passes since having gender-affirming surgery, with this decreasing by 8% each year (Bränström & Pachankis, 2020). In a systematic review, it was found that individuals who completed surgery to affirm their gender showed improvements in their quality of life and mental health (Wernick et al., 2019). These results are similar to other findings showing hormone therapy and surgery to affirm one's gender are associated with improvements in gender dysphoria, quality of life, mental health, and sexual functioning (Murad et al., 2010).

Importance of Support

Any person who is experiencing a major life event will benefit from having the support of others. Whether the support comes from a provider, a friend, coworker, or family members, having someone to lean on in a difficult time is critical to being able to move through the situation. There are two researchers who have most extensively explored the need for support: Caitlyn Ryan and Kristina Olson. We will review the results of their research here.

First is Caitlyn Ryan, who leads the Family Acceptance Project (https://familyproject.sfsu.edu/) which is located at San Francisco State University. Ryan and colleagues have numerous publications that address the need for family support for LGBTQ+ youths. In 2009, Ryan and colleagues published a groundbreaking study that found links between family rejection and negative health outcomes (Ryan et al., 2009). Even though this seems like common sense, too many LGBTQ+ youths experience harsh consequences after coming out to their family members. This includes being kicked out of the home; experiencing physical, sexual, and emotional abuse; and needing to rely on street economies and *survival sex*. Survival sex happens when a person agrees to engage in a sexual encounter for the purpose of having a safe place to stay or hot meals. Although survival sex has associated risks (e.g., STIs, violence), it may be safer than living on the street. Adolescents who are living the reality of homelessness are missing critical supports. There is also a strong likelihood that LGBTQ+ adolescents who are experiencing homelessness are missing important developmental milestones. It is important to note that much of the work from the Family Acceptance Project has focused on the lives of LGB people.

Some trans youth experience violent reactions when they come out to their parents

Olson and colleagues (2016) explored the mental health of prepubescent trans children. They were aware that children who have socially transitioned are much more visible, yet little is known about their emotional well-being. Olson recruited 73 trans children whose gender identity was opposite to the sex they were assigned at birth. One of the limitations of this study is that children with nonbinary identities were not included. Results indicated that depression levels in socially transitioned children were not significantly different from those of the general population. However, trans participants reported elevated levels of anxiety. The main finding of Olson and colleague's work is that trans children who had supportive families had subclinical levels of mental health concerns. These youth who were supported by their families did not have significant differences in depression or anxiety compared to age and gender matched youth in a control group or to their own siblings.

It would seem obvious that a person who receives support will have better mental health outcomes. However, as we have tried to communicate in this volume, there are numerous ways that trans people experience discrimination, mistreatment, and violence from a young age. Some of the violence comes at the hands of the very people who are supposed to care for us (e.g., parents). We will explore trauma in Section 4.4.1. Trauma can have far-reaching implications for the abused person.

Trans people are likely to have better mental health when they receive support

Conclusions About Therapeutic Interventions

In concluding this section focused on therapeutic approaches, we can say with some confidence that, even though the literature in this area is in an emerging stage, the qualities of therapeutic interventions that are helpful have the ability to make significant, positive impacts on trans clients. We have promising avenues for future research which will need to explore the effectiveness of specific interventions using RCTs. Furthermore, the research on gender-affirming medical care and social affirmation of one's gender indicates that there are significant positive benefits to supporting trans people in living a life that is in line with their affirmed gender identity.

4.3 Variations of the Method: Letter Writing

Letter writing may be a critical part of your practice with trans clients given that they may be seeking your support in order to obtain gender affirming medical care, such as hormones or surgeries. Historically, this process has been associated with gatekeeping (Budge, 2015; Budge & dickey, 2016). It is not the case that mental health providers sought this role (dickey, 2020), rather they were placed in this role because medical providers were seeking assurance that a trans client was emotionally stable prior to initiating medical care (e.g., hormone treatment or surgery). Regardless of how a mental health provider began conducting this type of care, there are a number of considerations that one should keep in mind in writing these letters (see Appendix 6 for sample letters).

> **Trans people often find the process of obtaining letters to be a significant barrier to care**

For clients who are existing therapy clients, this process may be incorporated into the therapy process. For other clients, it may be that this is the sole purpose of the clinical encounter. One barrier that many clients encounter is the possible need for multiple letters of support for transition services. Clients who are seeking breast or chest surgery need a single letter from a provider with at least a master's degree level of training according to the WPATH SOC.

If the client is seeking genital surgery, two letters are required according to the WPATH SOC (WPATH, 2012). The requirement for letters can add to the length of time that clients may be delayed in their gender affirmation, in addition to increasing the cost of the process. Trans individuals have been shown to be more likely to lack insurance coverage compared with cisgender people, encounter more issues with employment access and maintenance, and are more likely to live in poverty compared with cisgender people (James et al., 2016). Given this, psychologists may have clients who need letters of support provided at low cost or for free. We realize that one's ability to provide low or no fee services for letters of support will vary widely and be somewhat context dependent. If you have a client in need of a low or no fee service and are unable to do this, it may be worth exploring referral options such as to providers listed on the Gender Affirming Letter Access Project's website (https://thegalap.org/). The important thing to consider is how to best facilitate your clients' access to care.

> **You may need to help clients find affordable options for letters of support for their gender affirmation process**

When contacted by clients about a letter of support for medical gender affirmation, it is best to clearly and transparently describe the process

– including your general approach to the evaluation, a general sense of the number of sessions you anticipate needing with the client, and how you will provide the letter (e.g., to the client, directly to the provider). If you are not willing to write a letter for a client, you must ensure that they are aware of this.

In most cases, an evaluation for a letter of support can be completed in a single session. In this session, you can begin by sharing your background and education about trans people's experiences and your general view about the process. For instance, in discussing the purpose of the evaluation, you can share some of the following to set up a supportive and empowering clinical context:

- Acknowledge that your goals for treatment are to facilitate the client's access to care.
- Express a willingness to answer any questions throughout the process and to explain the reasoning for any of the questions asked if the client would like more information.
- Be transparent about the topic areas that will be covered in the evaluation and how these are needed in the letter so as to adequately address the requests of the medical provider.
- Provide an overview of your education and experience working with trans people; share your pronouns in your introduction.
- Make an explicit statement that you respect the range of gender experiences that trans people have and that you do not have expectations that the client has a binary narrative about their trans experience.
- Express your belief in the autonomy of trans people to make decisions about their bodies and gender experiences and that, as such, you do not adhere to existing stereotypes about trans people, such as their having, for example, known from a young age that they were trans.
- Acknowledge the history of the field of psychology and its role in gatekeeping and how this may make clients understandably worried about the process but that you will do your best to be transparent and supportive of the client.

Requiring an extensive number of sessions before writing a letter of support inappropriately delays trans clients' care

Medical providers will also likely have specific elements that they would like covered in the letter that you provide. It is helpful to contact the medical provider to inquire about what they would like covered in the letter and any specific formatting requirements. This will help ensure that you provide the strongest letter possible for the client and result in a lower likelihood of the client needing the letter revised or having to seek out a new letter writer.

The evaluation begins by getting to know more about the client's demographics and other aspects of identity that provide context for understanding their lived experiences. Following this, it is helpful to get an overview of the client's gender history. This can include the background information about how they currently identify, how long they have identified this way, changes over their lifetime, and other related questions. The psychologist should also assess for whether the client meets criteria for gender dysphoria, given that this diagnosis is often needed for insurance companies to provide the appropriate coverage for medical gender affirmation services. In beginning this discussion about symptoms aligning with the DSM-5 diagnosis of gender dysphoria, it may be helpful to start by explaining that this may be needed for insurance coverage and that the provider understands that much of the distress trans

A client's gender history may be very different than what you might have expected

people experience is a product of societal rejection and marginalization. It can help to make explicit that as a provider, you do not believe that being trans is a form of mental illness. This type of statement can help the client to feel more comfortable sharing with you their gender experience.

Psychologists should explore other ways in which the client has affirmed their gender in the past, such as through social affirmation steps like going by a name that fits their gender, changing their pronouns, and modifying their appearance. The client may have taken steps to legally affirm their gender through a legal name or gender marker change. Finally, there may have been other steps that the client has taken to affirm their gender through medical means (e.g., hormone blockers, hormones, surgeries).

In discussing the desired medical gender affirmation that a client is seeking, potential questions can cover the knowledge that the client has about the procedure, desired effects in reducing gender dysphoria, how this will help in their gender affirmation, and desired effects from the planned procedure. Psychologists can also inquire about any hesitations, fears, or concerns so that they can help clients to navigate these concerns without feeling as though they are risking their transition. A discussion of the risks or potential side effects will also help clients to think through their readiness for the services they are seeking. Finally, discussing recovery plans (if relevant) can help clients in preparing for any caretaking needs or logistical concerns that may impact their care.

> Recovery plans are critical as some surgical procedures can have significant, even life-threatening, side effects

Psychologists may not be entirely familiar with the range of medical procedures available for medical gender affirmation. As such, it is important that they seek out more information to build their knowledge about medical care (hormones and surgeries), common timelines associated with this care (e.g., the length of time for effects from hormones), any preparation that is needed for surgeries (e.g., hair removal, cessation of hormone treatment), common complications of the care, and the proper aftercare. Psychologists can gain such knowledge from reading (APA, 2015; Kauth & Shipherd, 2018; WPATH, 2012), attending training courses (Fenway Health's Advancing Excellence in Transgender Care conference; https://www.lgbthealtheducation.org/conferences/advancing-excellence-in-transgender-health/; see Appendix 3), or through consultation with medical providers as needed. If psychologists are uninformed, their discussions with clients will be less useful in supporting them through their medical gender affirmation. A list of potential conferences for psychologists who want to learn more about working with trans clients is provided in Appendix 7.

> It is important to understand the types and severity of symptoms clients are experiencing

Psychologists are also tasked with evaluating the presence and severity of other mental health concerns that may be impacting the client. Psychologists can screen for other concerns, such as depression, anxiety, suicidality, eating disorders, trauma, psychosis, substance use, and other potential diagnoses. Psychologists will want to understand the specific symptoms that clients are experiencing, the level of severity, and the degree to which these symptoms are impacting the client's functioning. Psychologists should also inquire about any health conditions that are impacting the client, implications for their gender affirmation process, medications, and general engagement in medical care. As stated earlier in this volume, simply having a mental health condition is not a reason for denying transition-related care.

Psychologists can also inquire about other health conditions that the client experiences and the possibilities of this being relevant to their gender-affirming medical care. For instance, surgeons may require that clients be under a certain body mass index (BMI) prior to surgery. Another example is surgeons usually require that clients stop smoking. Psychologists can assist clients in coming up with action plans to obtain their goals of gender-affirming medical care. Psychologists should also obtain information about other medications that clients are taking.

Finally, psychologists can explore interpersonal supports, stressors and sources of marginalization, and strengths for the client. These supports can be helpful in managing oppression, other mental health issues, or recovery from surgeries. Community connectedness with other trans people helps to bolster positive views of trans individuals and can decrease internalized stigma. In wrapping up the evaluation, the psychologist should clearly explain how they will proceed with writing the letter and any additional steps that are needed.

Be clear and transparent with clients about your process for letter writing

In terms of the actual letter, it is important to seek information from the medical provider and the insurance company to make sure that the necessary information they require is included in the letter. The following list gives the elements of a letter that are typically necessary for a referral for medical care:
- Your qualifications for conducting the assessment and licensure information
- The length of time you have worked with the client and dates of appointments
- Diagnosis of gender dysphoria (if required)
- A statement that this care is medically necessary for the client
- Relevant demographic information
- Brief summary of gender-related history information
- Your assessment regarding any other co-occurring mental health issues and whether these are reasonably well-controlled
- Your assessment of whether the client has the capacity to consent to treatment
- Client's understanding of the procedures, risks and benefits, outcomes, and your view of their readiness for this medical care
- Relevant information about supports available to the client
- Your willingness to be contacted for additional information if needed

The letter should be written on your professional letterhead and signed. You should communicate with the provider about how the letter will be delivered (e.g., fax, mail) and get the appropriate releases of information.

Don't forget to have your client sign a release granting permission to talk with another provider

4.4 Problems in Carrying Out Treatments

In this section, we will explore a number of challenges that you may face in working with trans clients. Of note, although these might be difficult situations, there is nothing about them that is inherently problematic. Rather, these are scenarios in which treatment may become more complex. Each of these situations has the potential to have influenced your clients and their loved ones.

4.4.1 Trauma

Trauma can be acute, chronic, or complex – all of which have implications for affirming care

Many trans people have a history of trauma. Usually, we think of trauma in terms of experiencing or witnessing a life-threatening situation. Trans people may certainly have had this type of experience, but there are many other ways a trans person experiences trauma. Trauma can be considered to be acute (within the 3 days after the event up to 1 month), chronic (lasting longer than a month after the incident), or complex. The National Child Traumatic Stress Network (2021) defines complex trauma as having been exposed to multiple traumatic experiences; these experiences may have occurred early in life, or the trauma (abuse) was carried out by a person who fills the role of caregiver for the person. For trans people, abuse in childhood may be related to the ways they expressed their gender in the home or in other areas of their life.

Trauma is common for trans people

Experiences of trauma for trans people may include sexual abuse in childhood, sexual assault, puberty, or intimate partner violence. In a study designed to explore "the association between social stress and health" (Reisner et al., 2016, p. 512), participants reported that they experienced discrimination from others related to their gender identity and/or expression, how masculine or feminine they appeared, their sexual orientation, the sex they were assigned at birth, and their age. In this same study, participants had elevated results on measurements of childhood abuse at age < 15 years, intimate partner violence, social transition, high levels of "visual gender nonconformity" (p. 517), and unstable housing. It is easy to see how the discrimination and violence that is experienced by trans people includes all domains of their life.

Military sexual assault (MSA) occurs in the lives of trans and cisgender service members. Beckman and colleagues (2018) found that of the 221 veterans who participated in their study, 17.2% had experienced MSA. Trans men were more likely to have experienced MSA (30%) than had trans women (15.2%). Having experienced MSA was also related to having been sexually assaulted as an adult and experiences of distal minority stress. Similar results were found in a study by Lindsay and colleagues (2016). They found that 15% of their sample had experienced MSA. Those service members were more likely to have clinically significant levels of depression or a personality disorder.

Nearly everyone in a study of trauma in trans people reported having experienced trauma

Shipherd and colleagues (2011) conducted a cross-sectional study of the traumatic experiences of trans people. Ninety-eight percent of participants reported having had one potentially traumatic event (Shipherd et al., 2011) in their lifetime, and 91% reported having experienced multiple PTEs. (PTE refers to any event that could be traumatic in nature.) Notable among the sample of trans women is that 17.8% showed clinical levels of PTSD, and 64% were experiencing clinical levels of depression.

Complex PTSD can look like borderline personality disorder – a differential diagnosis will be important

Richmond and colleagues (2012) offer a framework for understanding the types of trauma that trans people experience. They use a WHO model that clusters discrimination and violence as (a) interpersonal, (b) self-directed, or (c) collective (Krug et al., 2002). Trans people may experience one or all of these types of trauma in their lifetime. Richmond and colleagues report on the differences between *simple* and *complex* PTSD. Simple PTSD requires that the client have directly observed or been part of a traumatic event, and that simple trauma can be resolved through short-term approaches. At this time, there is no diagnostic difference between simple and complex PTSD. Complex PTSD can manifest with

> (a) difficulties in identity, (b) inability to foster stable relationships, (c) stress-related somatization, (d) inability to modulate emotional states, (e) alterations in consciousness and dissociation, (f) difficulty maintaining boundaries and personal safety, and (g) alterations in meaning making and spirituality. (Richmond et al., 2012, p. 46)

Interpersonal functioning is a central concept regarding complex PTSD. Other aspects of complex PTSD include that this mistreatment may come from a caregiver (e.g., parent, guardian), and it is not a single experience but rather the result of multiple assaults. Richmond and colleagues note the lack of literature that describes how to work with trans people let alone those who are survivors of trauma. They offer the following suggestions (a) develop a safe environment, (b) assess and address multiple types of violence, (c) connect the client with social support as it is comfortable for the client, (d) prepare clients for possible difficult interactions with health care professionals, (e) use inclusive language and paperwork, (f) address safety and self-care, (g) help clients learn to trust themselves, (h) engage clients in self-reflective interventions inside and outside of therapy, (i) examine your biases about gender and gender norms, (j) advocate for trans survivors of trauma, (k) train graduate students to work as advocates, (l) educate other mental health providers, (m) engage in prevention services, (n) advocate with policy makers about the rights of trans survivors, and (o) develop and initiate transpositive research (Richmond et al., 2012, pp. 51–53). Although these approaches were developed for work with trans survivors of trauma, they are applicable to any care that is offered to trans clients.

Helping trans clients to trust themselves is an important part of our work

When a trans person experiences an endogenous puberty (i.e., puberty that is consistent with the sex a person was assigned at birth), they may find this to be very distressing and it can particularly interact with past trauma exposures. The distress may relate to the ways that the client feels their body is betraying them. Stressors include breast growth and menarche (and continued menses) in trans masculine people, and for trans feminine people, the lowering of the pitch of their voice and male pattern baldness. These secondary sex characteristics and experiences can have negative implications for trans people that continue throughout their life. These experiences may impact trans individuals in terms of their experiences of other traumatic events.

4.4.2 Trans Clients in Rural Locations

Trans clients in rural areas face additional challenges. In their systematic review of the literature on health and health care for rural LGBTQ people, Rosenkrantz and colleagues (2017) found that rural individuals had higher rates of substance use (tobacco use, high-risk drinking, and other substances), challenges in getting HIV testing, and potential disparities in mental health. They also found that LGBTQ individuals in rural areas had more challenges in health care settings, such as encountering providers who are not competent or who are discriminatory. Walinsky and Whitcomb (2010) conducted a qualitative study that explored the experiences of trans people in rural settings. The four core themes from the study were vocation, personal change and coming out, acceptance, and identity. Walinsky and Whitcomb note the issues related to the job market in rural settings, the need for support in coming out to coworkers and family members, and the need for mental health providers to be well-trained if they would like to work with trans clients.

Trans people in rural areas face more minority stress, health challenges, and trouble finding care

Alarmingly, transgender people in rural areas may face even higher levels of suicidal ideation than their urban counterparts. Research with transgender individuals in Nebraska, a mostly rural state, found that 66% of transgender participants had seriously considered suicide in their lifetime (Irwin et al., 2014). Transgender individuals in their sample were 162% more likely to have considered suicide than cisgender LGBQ Nebraskans.

Research with transgender individuals across the US indicates worse mental health in rural areas. Transgender men have higher levels of somatization, anxiety, and depression, as well as lower self-esteem in rural areas in comparison with urban locations (Horvath et al., 2014). Rural transgender individuals also are less likely to be out to their personal contacts than cisgender LGBQ people (Whitehead et al., 2016). In addition, rural LGBTQ youths face more hostile school environments (Kosciw et al., 2015, 2020) and encounter more victimization as their levels of outness increase, in comparison with urban youths (Kosciw et al., 2009, 2020). Even within the rural state of Nebraska, there are differences across urban and rural subareas. Rural LGBTQ Nebraskans have lower levels of social engagement, less outness, and less self-acceptance, as well as higher levels of depression in comparison with urban LGBTQ people in Nebraska (Fisher et al., 2014). In sum, rural conservative states present climates that exacerbate the already staggering mental health disparities that exist for the transgender community, and this may be further amplified in rural areas within these states.

4.4.3 Autism Spectrum Disorder in Trans People

Some research shows a correlation between ASD and gender dysphoria

There have been reports that *autism spectrum disorder* (ASD) is found at higher rates in trans people, especially trans youths. In a letter to the editor, Turban (2018) makes the case for the myriad reasons the correlation exists between ASD and trans people. Turban points out that previous research has shown that trans youths score higher on measures of ASD as they age (de Vries et al., 2011). This is counter to the diagnostic criteria as set out in the DSM-5 (American Psychiatric Association, 2013), and typically a person will not experience heightened symptoms of ASD as they age. Turban explains that trans youths (and adults) face many challenges and difficulties after coming out to others being trans. This can easily lead to symptoms of depression and anxiety in addition to social awkwardness that trans people may be working through as they come into their affirmed gender identity. Turban (2018) refers to this as "social deficits secondary to social stress" (p. 4008).

Counter to Turban's argument are studies which have shown higher rates of ASD in trans people as compared with cisgender people. Warrier and colleagues (2020) set out to answer two questions: (a) do trans people have elevated rates of ASD diagnosis, and (b) do trans people have elevated autistic traits (e.g., systematizing, sensory hypersensitivity, reduced empathy). The study design included data from five, large data sets that were collected for different purposes; however, the central question was related to whether an individual has an ASD diagnosis. The results of the study indicated that trans people are overrepresented among those with an ASD diagnosis. Warrier and colleagues defend their results by stating that the diverse sample of data points (e.g., using five large data sets) makes it unlikely that the results represent false positives. They also state that the manner in which the data was analyzed through a comparison of odds ratios (OR) ensured that the resulting ORs were statistically significant. Third, the authors cite their use of sensitivity analysis with one of the data sets that did not show evidence of differences in the rates of ASD based on stated gender. Finally, they state that the ORs in their study are consistent with those found in other studies that show an association between ASD and having a diagnosis of gender dysphoria. Unlike other studies that have used a single question from the Childhood Behavior Checklist (CBCL) to determine if a person has a trans identity, the data sets used in this study collected demographic data from the participants. This allowed the research participants autonomy in identifying their gender.

Studies using a single item (#110) from the CBCL to determine gender identity are highly problematic

The end of the main section of the article hypothesizes why there are differences in ASD diagnosis between cisgender and transgender people. The first hypothesis addresses the ways that people with ASD tend not to conform to societal expectations. As such, they may be more likely to explore their gender and also not adhere to the gender binary. The second hypothesis suggests that the prenatal hormones that shape brain development also contribute to gender role behavior. The second hypothesis is similar to Turban's (2018). Warrier and colleagues (2020) suggest that the numerous stress-related experiences that a trans person might face would increase the likelihood that a trans person might develop other psychiatric concerns.

Thrower and colleagues (2020) conducted a systematic review of the literature related to ASD, attention-deficit/hyperactivity disorder (ADHD), and gender dysphoria. Out of 179 studies that were initially identified, only 30 were included in the review. Most of the articles that were included in the study used one or more autism rating scales (e.g., Social Responsiveness Scale, Autism Quotient, Diagnostic Interview for Social and Communication Disorders, Social Responsiveness Scale). Notably, only four of the studies used question 110 from the CBCL. That item asks whether the participant "wishes to be the opposite sex." As we have noted elsewhere in this volume, this single question is not a valid approach to determining if a person has a trans identity. The results of the various studies, some for adults and some for children, indicated that 6–26% of trans people had a diagnosis of ASD. Even though these rates exist in the literature, Thrower and colleagues (2020) caution the reader about drawing conclusions from the results. Specifically, they were concerned that most research which they were reporting did not have control groups, used self-reports, utilized retrospective chart review, and relied primarily on ASD screening tools rather than a full diagnostic interview. The authors also caution that although we have correlational data which seems to indicate a connection between ASD and trans people, much of the research is of low quality.

Reports of studies on ASD and gender dysphoria should be read with caution

Nobili and colleagues (2018) report the results of a promising study that addresses some of the problems noted in the previous studies. They used a case-control design in which each trans participant was matched with a cisgender person for their age and the sex they were assigned at birth. A total of 656 people participated in the study. Participants completed the Autism Spectrum Quotient – Short Version (AQ-short). Data collection for this study involved large groups of participants (4,070 cisgender people and 1,020 trans people) which were part of a longitudinal study. Although there were differences in the AQ-short scores, with trans people having higher scores, this result was not statistically significant. The only difference that was statistically significant was that trans people who were AFAB had the highest AQ-short results. This is possibly the only study in which trans and cisgender people were compared directly. This study was not without limitations, however. The authors point out that the prevalence of ASD in the cisgender group was significantly higher than is seen in the general population (33.2% in the cisgender study sample and 1.1% in the general population; Brugha et al., 2011). The finding that trans people AFAB have a higher likelihood of also having an ASD is consistent with previous research. The authors note the bias that exists, stating that ASD screening tools are more likely to indicate that a male individual has clinically significant ASD symptoms. When thinking about the results of this study and the fact that trans masculine and possibly nonbinary people were more likely to have ASD symptoms, it is hard to know how masculinity may have influenced the findings. Other limitations noted by the authors include the need to match participants on other demographic characteristics such as IQ and education level. The authors note that the cisgender sample relied on a snowball sampling technique which may also have contributed to the high number of cisgender people with ASD. Finally, trans and cisgender participants completed different versions of the AQ. Even so, the scores that were compared were based on the same set of questions.

> In a study, the differences in ASD scores between and cisgender participants were not significant

In addressing ASD in trans people, the best conclusion right now is that we do not yet have clear evidence that trans people are more likely to have an ASD. Results of some studies have been problematic in the manner in which the data were collected, the ways in which a person was deemed to be trans, and the lack of controlled comparisons. Most important to take away from this section is the importance of meeting our clients where they are. This means that we address the clinical concerns that are relevant for our clients and do not create a clinical concern where none exists.

> We do not yet have solid evidence of a connection between ASD and gender dysphoria

4.4.4 Co-Occurring Medical Concerns

One reason that trans people are not able to move forward with their transition is related to having one or more co-occurring medical concerns. Most guidelines or recommendations will state that treatment can commence provided there are no contraindications. Similar to the manner in which the SOC use the term "reasonably well-controlled," simply stating that there are no contraindications is not helpful to the reader. Bruessow and colleagues (2019) and others provide the suggestions as shown in Table 5. It is important to note the differences in the contraindication effects of hormones. No trans person wants to hear that they cannot start hormones; however, if they have a significant health condition that will be exacerbated by the use of hormones, it is important to

Table 5
Medical contraindications to hormone treatment

Treatment	Contraindication
Puberty blockers (GnRH analog)	Sensitivity to the medication
Testosterone	Pregnancy Coronary artery disease Androgen-sensitive breast cancer Active endometrial cancer Lipid disorders with cardiovascular complications[a] Cerebrovascular disease[a] Thromboembolic disease[a] Marked obesity[a] Poorly controlled diabetes[a] Poorly controlled hypertension[a] Clotting abnormalities[a] Active liver disease[a] Severe obstructive sleep apnea[a] Polycythemia[a] Active substance abuse[a] History of deep vein thrombosis[a]
Estradiol	Thromboembolism Thrombophlebitis Estrogen-dependent cancer Low bone mineral density[b] Cardiovascular disease[b]

Note. GnRH = gonadotropin releasing hormone. [a]Possible contraindication. [b]These contraindications are specific to trans women who are living with HIV. Based on Bruessow et al., 2019; King & Gamarel, 2020; Radix et al., 2016; Steinle, 2011.

help the client work through the attendant disappointment. If there are no medical contraindications, and the client has made an informed consent, there is no reason to delay the initiation of hormone treatment. Given that many psychologists are not intimately aware of these health conditions, this is something that the client will often need to talk about with the medical provider who is providing their transition-related care. Therapists may be in a position of gathering some information about health conditions but it is typically outside of our purview to provide guidance about medical health concerns like these. We may document concerns in letters of support and what clients are doing to manage these conditions to support them in their gender affirmation.

Little has been written about contraindications for surgical procedures. This may be due the fact that there is no difference in clinical concerns from what there would be for any other surgical procedure. Two things our clients need to be prepared for is the need to stop hormones and to stop smoking. Many people do not want to stop hormones, because they are concerned about the physical implications of doing so. Typically, this needs to happen about 2 weeks before and for no more than 2 weeks after surgery, if at all. Smoking cessation is more difficult. Depending on how long a person has been smoking, stopping may feel like an insurmountable task.

4.4.5 Persistence, Insistence, and Consistence

Although this text is written primarily with adults in mind, it is worth noting some specific concerns related to youth. It is not uncommon that a parent has questions about their child's declaration that they are not a girl or a boy, as assigned at birth. These questions should be expected, as they indicate that the parent(s) are engaged in their child's life. Some in the field have affirmed that "if a child is persistent, insistent, and consistent," then they are likely a trans person (Leibowitz, 2021). However, the discussion of persistence originates from flawed research that showed that not all children who present as trans in childhood will go on to transition later in life (Steensma et al., 2013). This research is seen as flawed by many in the field and thus the clinical utility of this understanding of youth is questionable. Steensma and colleagues report that children with lower intensity of persistence are less likely to be trans. This is known as *desistence*. The main concern with the research about desistence is that the researchers assumed that a person did not transition if they did not seek follow-up care. There are any number of reasons a child (and their family) may not follow up care (e.g., moved from the area, sought care elsewhere), and the authors did not take this into consideration. As such, this research may not fully represent the experiences of trans youth.

Children and youth should also be supported in exploring their gender

Providers will need to work closely with the child and their family to ensure that the child or adolescent is getting the care they need (and deserve), is being treated well in school and other social settings (e.g., youth groups, church), and has a good understanding of the implications of moving forward with transition.

4.5 Multicultural Issues

There are, as of this writing, no clinical approaches that have been extensively validated via RCTs with trans people. Budge and colleagues (2021) have obtained promising results in their work; both of their treatment groups reported statistically significant differences with their treatment approaches – one that was generally trans affirming and the other that included the aspects of the first, with the addition of MST. Budge and colleagues reported that of the 10 participants in their study, only two reported a multiracial background. Seven of the 10, though, reported having a nonbinary identity. As Budge and colleagues move forward with studying the effectiveness of this treatment method, it will be critical to ensure that trans people from diverse racial backgrounds are included in their research.

Existing studies on evidence-based practices with trans clients have relied on primarily white samples

Much of the research with trans individuals more broadly has been conducted with primarily white samples. One of the reasons for this is the reliance on the Internet for data collection. Even though online surveys may seem to be the best approach to accessing otherwise hard-to-reach participants, study after study has shown that 70% to 80% of participants are white. This will need to be addressed so that our knowledge about affirming interventions takes into account the lives of trans people of color and other intersecting aspects of identity (e.g., disability, religious beliefs, nationality, immigration status).

Some might say that the ideal course of study to include information about trans people in the training curriculum would be a course addressing multicultural issues. Although there is some value to that statement, ideally, issues that impact trans people should be addressed across the curriculum.

Curricula for training should include course topics such as career counseling, personality and cognitive assessment, clinical training, and group counseling. Recently, a group of students and professionals developed a resource that provides a plethora of ideas for how to include trans identities across the curriculum (Society of Counseling Psychology, 2020). Importantly, the guide begins with a number of resources that address making the classroom safe.

> **The needs of trans people should be addressed across the curriculum, without pathologization**

4.5.1 Intersectionality

It is essential that psychologists integrate an intersectional approach to their work (Budge & Moradi, 2018). Trans clients will be exposed to varying levels of stigma depending on other aspects of their identity, such as race, and providers will need to understand any given client's specific social location and how this shapes their lived experiences. This intersectional approach can be integrated across client's social experiences and should be included in case conceptualizations which integrate a resilience focus that explicitly addresses other aspects of identity. We encourage psychologists to do a deeper dive into intersectionality to support their growth in this area (e.g., Crenshaw, 1991).

> **Understanding the aspects of identity that shape a client's life is essential to all affirming care**

Trans people experience discrimination in many aspects of their life. This includes SDOH such as unemployment, food insecurity, housing insecurity, a lack of access to competent and affirmative health care, and myriad forms of discrimination and violence. Thomas and colleagues (2017) highlight the challenges that trans people face. First, there is a need to fill the gaps in the literature that address social determinants and trans health. Second, barriers to care and the manner in which trans people access care need to be better understood. Third, the ways in which social exclusion impacts trans people must be understood at the individual, intrapersonal, and societal levels (Thomas et al., 2017).

> **SDOH impact the lives of trans people, especially those with multiple marginalizations**

For trans people who have other marginalized identities – for example, Black, Indigenous, and people of color (BIPOC), ability status, and immigration status – the difficulties are multiplied. Having an intersecting marginalized identity will certainly increase the likelihood of mistreatment. This may not be limited to how a trans person is treated in their typical day-to-day life. Many trans people are mistreated in health care settings, and psychologists are sometimes part of the problem.

We discussed harm reduction in Section 2.5: Harm Reduction. It is possible that trans people, including BIPOC individuals will seek care and will share with their provider that they have been obtaining their hormones from sources

Ensuring clients have a safe supply of hormones is critical

other than a medical provider. This might include purchasing hormones over the Internet or buying them from an acquaintance or friend without knowledge of the source of the medications. Providing a referral for this client to a provider who will manage the client's hormones ensures that the client has access to a safe supply of hormones. Because of the ways that trans BOPIC experience more negative social determinants of health and more mistreatment from providers, they may more frequently seek care that has not been medically supervised out of a need resulting from social oppression.

Table 6
Social determinants of health experienced by trans BIPOC

	Latino/a	American Indian	African American	Asian, Native Hawai'ian, Pacific Islander
Poverty	43%	41%	38%	32%
Unemployed	21%	23%	20%	10%
Homelessness	31%	57%	42%	21%
Sexual assault	48%	65%	53%	41%
Uncomfortable with police	59%	59%	67%	58%
Negative experience with health provider	32%	50%	34%	26%
HIV+	1.6%	2.0%	6.7%	Unknown
Psychological distress	45%	46%	41%	39%

Note. BIPOC = Black, Indigenous, and people of color. Based on James et al., 2016.

As we think about cultural issues, intersectionality is one of the most important concepts as various aspects of identity and how they come together have significant impacts on the lives of trans people. For example, in the general population approximately 0.3% are living with HIV. Among trans people, that number is 1.4%. Black trans people have reported HIV infection levels at 6.7%. Black trans women have reported HIV infection rates of 19% (James et al., 2016). These disparate rates of living with HIV are caused by various social determinants of health. In Table 6 we describe other ways that trans BIPOC are adversely impacted by social determinants of health when they have intersecting marginalized identities. Experiencing multiple negative social determinants of health has the potential to be debilitating for a person.

4.6 Importance of Interrogating Your Gender

There have been numerous calls for psychologists to interrogate their gender as part of their preparedness for working with trans clients (APA, 2015; Chang et al., 2018).

Many years ago, Peggy McIntosh (1989) published an article that addressed the ways she was able to walk in the world without there being any restriction based on the color of her skin; or because she had white privilege. In the same light, the first author of the present work developed a similar listing of the ways that cisgender people can walk in the world and not receive mistreatment because of their gender. These are shown in the following list of statements to consider, based on the work of Peggy McIntosh (1989):

- I do not have to worry that someone will tell me that I am in the wrong restroom.
- I do not have to worry about whether I will receive competent care if I am not able to tell a doctor about my gender.
- On first meeting me, no one asks me about my genitals.
- I can usually count on another person using the correct pronoun.
- I do not need to be concerned that others will assume I am unfit to be a parent because of my gender identity.
- I am not excluded from employment or social services because of my gender.
- I do not have to worry that I will be harassed by a police officer because my gender expression is different from the sex listed on my identification.
- I do not have to worry that I will be pulled aside by the US Transportation Security Administration because my X-ray image is not consistent with what was expected.
- I do not have to "out" myself on an employment application when someone asks if I have ever used another name.
- I do not have to worry about whether I can receive health care for the organs that are present in (or absent from) my body.
- I do not fear for my safety when I am in public because my gender might be misunderstood by another.
- I am not afraid to talk to another person about what it means to have a gender identity.

Interrogating your gender should start early in your clinical practice. Whether this happens with supervision when you are a trainee or in a consultation group after you are independently licensed, we must all attend to the biases we have about gender. Our clients deserve to work with psychologists who have made an effort to understand their inherent biases. The goal is not to eliminate biases (although that would be helpful) but rather to understand how our thoughts and beliefs about gender may get in the way of our work with trans clients. For example, if we hold a belief that men are supposed to be strong and hold power in relationships with others; how will we work with a trans woman who is coming out and will need to give up these expressions of male privilege?

Interrogating your gender is a personal and necessary process for those who work with trans people

Gender roles are learned at a young age

We learn from a young age about the many ways that men and women are supposed to behave in the world. Never do we hear about how a nonbinary person is supposed to fit into this schema. Further, we rarely, if ever, hear our parents talk about the option of being trans later in life. Some might say this is one of the ways that parents protect their children. This is not how trans and nonbinary children are protected. Silence on the topic of gender and gender identity is complicit with adhering to cisnormative ideas about gender. Our children deserve better. Trans and nonbinary people deserve better.

4.7 Problematic Treatments

4.7.1 Conversion Therapy

Briefly stated, conversion therapy is a harmful approach to working with LGBTQ+ people in a manner that attempts to "cure" the client of their sexual orientation or gender identity. Notably, this approach is only used with sexual and gender minorities and not with their cisgender, heterosexual counterparts. This approach has also been referred to as sexual orientation change efforts (also known as SOCE) or gender identity change efforts (GICEs).

Ex-gay ministries (religious groups built around SOCE) have a complicated past. Sadly, many people, mostly gay men, were mistreated through ex-gay ministries and exposed to SOCE. Clients lost their autonomy in these treatment approaches and were given false hope of treatment effectiveness. Conversion therapy has not only been about people who are sexual minorities. Versions of this approach, which may not always have been religious, were also used to treat gender minorities.

GICE is an approach that is harmful and ineffective

Turban and colleagues (2019) examined the data collected through the US Transgender Survey (James et al., 2016) to explore the long-term effects of GICEs. Their research shows that 19.6% of respondents ($n = 3,896$) who ever talked with a provider about their gender identity indicated having been treated with GICE at some point in their lifetime. This experience of having a mental health provider attempt to talk them out of being trans happened to 17% of those who were AMAB and 21% of those AFAB (Turban et al., 2019). These individuals had higher rates of severe psychological distress and elevated risk of a suicide attempt. A recent resolution by APA (2021) contains the strongest language the Association has ever offered on the topic of conversion therapy. Their statement includes the following, "GICE … puts individuals at significant risk of harm, … APA opposes the idea that incongruence between sex and gender is a mental disorder, … and … APA promotes professional training in gender affirming practices" (APA, 2021). Although this is the strongest statement yet regarding GICE, APA still falls short in not labeling the practice to be unethical.

What is especially problematic about conversion therapy is that the primary targets of this treatment are adolescents. Adolescence is a vulnerable time of life for any person. It is even more so for those who have questions about their gender. Some trans people report having been exposed to conversion therapy before the age of 10 (Turban et al., 2019). In recent years, 20 states and the District of Columbia have enacted laws that ban conversion therapy for minors (MAP, 2021). North Carolina and Puerto Rico have partial bans against conversion therapy. It is important to note that in North Carolina it is against the law to use state funds to support conversion therapy (MAP, 2021). Alabama, Georgia, and Florida are in a federal circuit court case that includes a preliminary injunction that prevents enforcement of conversion therapy bans (MAP, 2021). There are 26 states and four territories that are silent about the use of conversion therapy. This puts many young people at risk of a treatment that has no evidence for effectiveness and has been shown numerous times to harm those who are subjected to conversion therapy treatment. Laws banning conversion therapy are targeted at minors. The reason for this is that minors are not able to consent to the approach. Adults may choose to engage in this type of approach, and because they are able to consent to care, there are no laws or regulations preventing them from doing so. If you have adult clients who have explored this type of approach, you may need to assist the client with understanding how GICE has impacted their sense of self and the ways they understand gender.

Despite the clear harm caused by conversion therapy, it is still legal in many areas

Likely the most useful resource that is currently available is a SAMHSA publication that was released in 2015. This resource takes a hard look at conversion therapy (also known as reparative therapy). SAMHSA is very clear about the ways that this approach to clinical work is harmful. For example, SAMHSA recognizes that little research has been conducted on this topic; however, what has been conducted has *never* shown that mental health treatment can change a person's gender identity or sexual orientation. They also state that "interventions aimed at a fixed outcome … are coercive, can be harmful, and should not be a part of behavioral health treatment" (SAMHSA, 2015, p. 1).

Ending Conversion Therapy **by SAMHSA is an easily accessible resource**

The SAMHSA report set out to create a professional consensus on the harm that conversion therapy represents to SGM children and adolescents. The report offers 10 statements related to gender identity and gender expression. Like the APA guidelines (APA, 2015), SAMHSA states that variations in gender identity and expression are normal variations of the human experience and are not evidence of a mental health concern. They also make clear that gender is not binary. SAMHSA discusses the possible trajectory of youths based on their age and whether they might develop a trans identity. SAMHSA cautions providers against holding a "prescriptive goal" (SAMHSA, 2015, p. 13) for treatment. The biggest concern here is the expectation that the youth client is not trans. Ultimately, providers should trust clients and honor their stories rather than projecting their beliefs onto clients.

SAMHSA then offers several statements addressing appropriate therapeutic interventions. This begins by acknowledging the ways in which gender diverse youths are vulnerable and the importance of ensuring that parents have "accurate scientific information" (SAMHSA, 2015, p. 13).

GICE have been used to harm trans people for decades

Information can be used to help parents make decisions that are in the best interest of their child. For pre-pubertal children, it is recommended that a thorough assessment be conducted. This can help to gain a greater understanding of the kinds of emotional distress that a child is experiencing. It is recommended that peripubertal adolescents be afforded access to puberty suppression treatment. It is beyond the scope of this volume to discuss this process of affording access to puberty suppression treatment, in great detail. Readers are encouraged to review the work of Johanna Olson-Kennedy (also known as Johanna Olson) for more information about this medical intervention.

Puberty suppression can be used for peripubertal trans adolescents

Prior to initiating puberty suppression, it is important to conduct an assessment for the purpose of understanding the emotional needs of the adolescent. Pubertal and postpubertal adolescents may require similar assessments.

If these youths are considering a medical (or physical) transition, it will be important to discuss risks and benefits of treatment and to have a ready source of providers who will engage in care. Often, these providers can be found in major cities at a children's hospital. This final recommendation for pubertal and postpubertal adolescents comes with a caution about the ways that withholding treatment can exacerbate gender dysphoria and other emotional reactions (SAMHSA, 2015). Unless there are issues with the trans adolescent's parents consenting to treatment, it is possible to start a teenager on hormones. If the adolescent's parents are not supportive or if there is mixed support (e.g., one parent is supportive, but the other is not), your work with the client will be focused on helping them to manage the emotional distress that is associated with not being respected in their gender and having to wait to access care.

The SAMHSA (2015) resource is invaluable for providers who work with SGM youths. It provides a significant compilation of the extant literature addressing the needs of SGM youths as well as the ways that conversion therapy is a deeply problematic clinical approach. Given that 20 states and the District of Columbia have enacted laws banning conversion therapy with minors, it is important that this clinical approach be discontinued (MAP, 2021).

4.7.2 Rapid Onset Gender Dysphoria

ROGD is not supported by science and claiming it to be legitimate is harmful to trans people

There have been attempts to frame arguments that call into question the legitimacy of trans people's identities as "science." One notable example of this being *rapid onset gender dysphoria* (ROGD). At its core, ROGD characterizes gender dysphoria and trans identities as a "social contagion" and has been weaponized against individuals who are AFAB and disclose a trans or nonbinary identity. Proponents of ROGD claim that some youths start to identify as trans as a product of their peer group, having contact with other trans people, and social media.

Littman published an article in 2018 claiming to find evidence for ROGD (Littman, 2018), yet there were many flaws with this study, and within respected professional organizations and groups, it is generally viewed as having been debunked. A few of the key issues with this study were recruitment bias, sample bias, and inaccurate interpretation of findings. Participants were recruited from websites and groups that are known for invalidating the experiences of trans people, and which are viewed as holding antitransgender bias. The sample did not include youths themselves and instead relied on parent reports about their children, which is inherently biased. Finally, the interpretation of finding support for ROGD was problematic given the methodological flaws of the study. A more extensive critique can be found in Restar (2020).

ROGD is harmful and damaging to trans people and specifically trans youths. This is a term that supports questioning the legitimacy of trans youths' identities and offers hesitant parents a reason to pathologize their children.

The dangers of endorsing ROGD as legitimate are clear. This may lead to hesitancy in allowing trans youths to affirm their gender through social means, although we know that when youths are supported in their identity they have better mental health outcomes (Olson et al., 2016). This may also lead to the harmful internalization of stigma as youths are told that their identities are not "real" and are a product of social influence. This can significantly hamper the identity development of trans youths who are already living in a world where constant invalidation of trans identities is the norm.

We operate from the base understanding that trans people know themselves, that no provider will have better insight about a trans person's identity than the client does, and that it is not possible to "catch" being trans from peers or social media. As such, we wish to emphasize that it is problematic and a misrepresentation of the scientific evidence to attempt to legitimize ROGD. This is not a diagnosis. The publications on ROGD have been challenged, and it has essentially been debunked.

ROGD is *not* a reputable scientific concept

Given this, it would be counter to the empirical evidence, what is known about affirming and ethical care with trans people, and best practices to encourage screening for ROGD or to attempt to perpetuate this type of misinformation. Treating ROGD as legitimate, and encouraging families or other providers to do so causes harm to trans youths, trans communities more broadly, and to the broader mental health profession. There have been many providers who have been working to build trust between themselves and trans communities and when mental health professionals perpetuate such harmful practices, it leads to larger ruptures and, understandably, mistrust from trans clients. When trans clients cannot trust that their identities will not be questioned by mental health professionals, it damages the work that has been done in the field to advance affirming, culturally responsive care.

Providers who treat ROGD as legitimate cause harm to clients and misrepresent empirical evidence

5

Case Vignettes

Eliza

Eliza, like many trans people, has a significant trauma history

Eliza is a 28-year-old who was AMAB. Eliza completed high school and has about 25 college credits. She identifies as a Black trans woman. Her trauma history is quite significant. She scored 9 out of 10 on the Adverse Childhood Experiences (ACE; Felitti et al., 1998) assessment. Eliza was born in the US, and her parents are first generation US citizens. Their respective parents immigrated to the US from Jamaica.

Until recently, Eliza lived with a cisgender male partner (named Liam) for 2 years. They lived in an apartment together, but the lease was only in his name. When she first moved in, this seemed like an acceptable living situation. That was due in part to Eliza not having had a stable home prior to meeting Liam. Eliza mostly stayed at home and took care of household chores. Liam had not forbidden Eliza from working, but he assured her that he would take responsibility for providing for her.

Stable housing has been a challenge

Eliza was referred by her physician. Eliza had been to see this provider to get a refill on her medication to treat a hepatitis B infection. The physician asked Eliza how things were going for her. The physician had noticed that Eliza's appearance was more disheveled than usual. Eliza admitted that she and her partner had recently broken up, which resulted in her losing a place to live. Eliza stated that she has exhausted the kindness of her friends and has been living on the street for about a month. She does not have a job, and since she has not been in the workforce for over 2 years, she does not believe she has the skills needed to find meaningful work.

Assessing Eliza's Need for Support

An ill-informed provider may believe that they should start with an assessment to determine their client's gender. There are no assessments that can be used to determine whether a person is trans. Deogracias and colleagues (2007) developed an assessment that on face value seems to assess whether or not a person has a trans identity. Their assessment measure, titled the *Gender Identity/Dysphoria Questionnaire for Adolescents and Adults* (GIDYQ-AA), was designed as a means of exploring whether a person was experiencing questions about their gender identity. One problem with the GIDYQ-AA is that it was created as a measure to assess binary conceptualizations of gender. This means that if a trans person has a nonbinary identity, this assessment tool would not be useful. A further concern is that the developers believed that it was important to anchor the scale in the client's sex assigned at birth. This type of thinking is problematic as it fails to honor a person's lived experience of gender. This scale is not, to the knowledge of the authors, used in clinical practice. It is good that this is the case. A provider could spend much less time and not risk alienating their client if they simply talked with the client about their gender history. This conversation might be framed by the diagnostic criteria for gender dysphoria, but that conceptualization is not requisite.

> A clinical interview can tell you more about a person's gender than any specific scale

The SOC (WPATH, 2012) call for a psychosocial assessment for clients who want to initiate hormones or have surgery. A psychosocial assessment is used to ascertain the needs, risks, and protective factors experienced by a client, regardless of their gender identity. In the case of Eliza, there was no need to "assess" her identity as a trans person or her readiness for gender affirming medical care as this was not the focus of the appointment. As we have discussed, hyperfocusing on the medicalization of trans people's experiences can be experienced as a microaggression if that is not what the client is coming in to discuss. It was important to explore the ways that her sense of self and safety are at risk. If they were, it would be important to connect Eliza with resources in the community that will honor her identity, while providing her with the resources she needs.

Prior to referring Eliza to a shelter for people who are experiencing homelessness, it would be necessary to determine whether the shelter would be a safe place for Eliza. Even though living on the street has inherent risk, being placed in a shelter and subsequently being required to share sleeping space with cisgender men may put Eliza at greater risk. If shelter staff see this as the only housing choice for Eliza, they are not likely to be responsive if Eliza is mistreated by other shelter residents.

> Psychologists should be mindful of referrals and whether they would be affirming of trans clients

Kai

Kai is a 21-year-old, Asian, genderqueer, pansexual individual who was AFAB (pronouns: they/them). Kai came to the clinic due to feelings of sadness, hopelessness, and anxiety. Kai is currently an undergraduate student and living on their campus in the women's dorms. In our conversation with Kai, they described feeling down most days, being worried about how others perceive them, feeling on edge when around others, and largely keeping to themselves in order to avoid social interactions. They also endorsed various physical symptoms of anxiety, such as feeling shaky, having trouble breathing, and experiencing tension. They have limited their showering to once a week as they are anxious about using the floor's shower space given that this is a women's dorm and a shared shower room. They also shared feelings of hopelessness and a heightened fear for their safety, particularly as an upcoming federal election included one candidate who had made repeated threats to trans people's safety.

Kai is not out to their parents about their gender, but is interested in moving forward with starting hormones to affirm their gender. They know that after this, there will be physical changes that will require them to have a conversation with their family and they are unsure how to navigate this. Although they do not have many supports in the local small college town, they travel to see friends in a larger city every couple of months. Most of these friends are also trans. Kai feels a sense of freedom when outside of the small town and away from college and, when they return, they feel a deep sense of vigilance and heightened anxiety about how others treat them.

In terms of school performance, Kai is majoring in gender studies and most of their classes are taught by professors who are affirming of trans people. Their professors in these classes ask for the names students want to go by and pronouns. In these classes, Kai is excelling, getting all A's. However, in other courses, Kai reports being misgendered by professors and peers and having their given name used on a regular basis. Kai mentioned in the intake that every time this happens, it feels like a "punch in the gut," and they have trouble focusing the rest of the class period. Kai has tried to talk with a few professors, but the negative response of one professor made them shut down emotionally, and they stopped advocating for themselves. In most courses outside of their major, Kai is having significant difficulty with their performance and grades. Kai's concerns are further elevated due to being on a need-based scholarship with a requirement that they keep above a certain GPA. Kai's family does not have the means to pay for college, and if they cannot pull up their grades within the next semester, they may lose their scholarship, jeopardizing their ability to continue in school. This high amount of pressure feels further immobilizing to Kai.

Therapeutic Approach With Kai

It is important for Kai to be provided with inclusive paperwork at the first visit, with spaces for their affirmed name and pronouns (see Section 2.6: Shaping the Therapeutic Dialogue). If there is a section for an emergency contact, it also would be important to discuss with Kai what name and pronouns to use if the need to contact others were to happen. For instance, if they provided their mother's information but are not out to her, then the provider may end up in a situation in which they out Kai to their family and place them in danger or further exacerbate their mental health concerns. If scales are administered, the provider would need to evaluate whether the items use binary language or are based on gendered norms. If so, the provider should find alternatives that may be less marginalizing (see Section 3.1: Assessment).

If a provider were to start working with Kai without taking into account the various social and contextual factors impacting their mental health, they may simply see a person struggling with social anxiety. They could even use approaches that may place Kai in danger or be invalidating, such as choosing exposure exercises that may be physically dangerous to trans people. Through some of the details provided above, it is clear that the social environment and marginalization plays a significant role in Kai's anxiety symptoms (see Section 2.1: Minority Stress Theory). In fact, when Kai is in spaces where they are affirmed, they feel relief and as though they can be present and engaged. In an initial intake, it would be imperative that a provider ask questions to understand how identity based experiences relate to the client's everyday life and mental health (see Section 2.6: Shaping the Therapeutic Dialogue). This could be done through means such as creating questions using Pamela Hays' ADDRESSING framework which encompasses age and generational influences, developmental or other disability, religion and spirituality, ethnic and racial identity, socio-economic status, sexual orientation, indigenous heritage, national origin, and gender (Hays, 2016), or through adapting your own intake to inquire about identity-based experiences. Through integrating these types of questions, the provider would have a more extensive case conceptualization and learn about key factors that are eliciting and maintaining Kai's symptoms, thereby strengthening the therapeutic relationship and having better therapy outcomes.

After the intake session, the provider could utilize the client case conceptualization form provided in the appendix as a way to organize information while taking into account Kai's context (see Section 4.2.2: Therapeutic Approaches). In this case, Kai reported a range of distal stressors. These include being misgendered daily, being told they were in the "wrong" bathroom at least weekly, someone putting a note with a racial slur under their dorm door last month, and a prior experience in high school where they were shoved into a wall by a peer who shouted homophobic and racial slurs at them.

At the proximal level, Kai endorsed a high degree of expectations of rejection. These seemed realistic based on many of their day-to-day experiences and the contextual factors surrounding Kai's life. It was important for the provider to not pathologize these expectations. They indeed seemed like reasonable and realistic expectations for a trans, genderqueer, Asian, pansexual person living in a women's dorm in a small, mostly white, college town. At the proximal level, Kai endorsed internalized stigma because of the messages they had received about trans people and as a product of their lived experiences. They also had some level of identity concealment in terms of their family of origin. This was simultaneously a source of stress and a protective strategy. They had to manage being misgendered by their family and felt distant from them due to not being able to be out to them. They had a reasonable expectation that their family would cut off contact with them if they came out. They were unprepared for this to happen at the time. In terms of the social narratives and lived environment in this case, Kai had been exposed to both positive and negative narratives of trans people's lives. Their gender studies program was very inclusive and their courses regularly acknowledged a range of gender experiences. They also had close friends who were trans, but they lived in a nearby city. Their other courses were very binary in terms of discussing gender, and they just completed an "abnormal psychology" course where the professor made sensationalizing and pejorative comments about trans people when discussing the gender dysphoria chapter. There were other students in the class who asked ignorant questions and the professor laughed along with them about how "confused" trans people were and all the "made up genders" out there.

At the broader societal level, Kai tries to stay engaged and aware about politics, but this is stressful. One of the candidates in the upcoming election regularly endorses transphobic views and has made several threats to trans people's safety. Kai also heard of two trans people of color being murdered over the past week. These social narratives about trans people perpetuate stigma and have led Kai to expect that their own life will likely be cut short if they affirm their gender. Other factors in the lived environment include living in the women's dorm, not having access to a private shower, Kai's state not having a gender neutral option on identification cards, and the school not having an affirmed name policy, which results in Kai being outed and misgendered on a daily basis. Finally, in terms of the relational context, Kai has few affirming connections locally, they have to travel to a larger city to spend time with affirming friends, they feel isolated from their family, and they lack a sense of community to other trans people as well as to other Asian individuals. Completing the associated case conceptualization form helped the provider to organize the details of the case and to find connections between the client's mental health and the underlying factors that may be influencing their symptoms as well as ways to bolster resilience.

The provider should seek clarity in the initial session as to whether Kai is seeking therapy or is seeking a letter of support for hormone therapy (or both). It is important to be clear on the provider's role from the start. In this case, Kai is looking for therapy right now but is hoping to pursue hormones in the next year or so. There is no need to conduct an evaluation or provide a letter of support until Kai is ready to pursue hormone therapy (see Section 4.3: Variations of the Method: Letter Writing). The provider can explore with Kai what topics they would like to discuss in therapy in preparation for starting hormones. Kai shared that sometimes they worry about starting hormones because they heard a cisgender person make statements about health-related side effects that were, in the provider's view, exaggerated and based in fear mongering. Kai shared they have some internal barriers, wherein they judge themselves and feel like they are "not trans enough" to start hormones. Treatment goals could be identified for this aspect of therapy, such as 1) learning more about the side effects of hormones, 2) identifying barriers to starting hormones (including internal beliefs, access to resources, etc.), 3) challenging internalized stereotypes about trans people to develop a more positive view of self, and 4) learning about the range of experiences and identities of trans people to develop a more positive view of self.

As outlined in the text, there is a lack of research on treatments that are specific to trans people's experiences (see Chapter 4: Treatment). The provider should seek out evidence-based approaches that match the presenting problems while making adaptations to ensure these interventions are affirming to trans clients. In Kai's case, it was clear that there were a variety of contextual factors that were negatively impacting their mental health. Using an empowerment framework, the provider could work with Kai to identify factors that could be changed to decrease anxiety symptoms. Kai identified the dorm and lack of private showers as a major concern. The university does not have gender inclusive housing but does offer single person rooms with private showers. Kai had heard about this, but always felt overwhelmed by the prospect of advocating for themselves to have a change in their living situation. The provider could use motivational interviewing techniques to explore the pros and cons of asking to be moved to a private dorm room vs. staying in their current living situation. As a result, Kai's openness to engaging in this self-advocacy increased. They still felt unprepared for how to go about seeking the change in housing, so the therapist provided some education about the appropriate offices to reach out to and did role plays in session to improve Kai's communication and self-advocacy skills. Given Kai's anxiety, the therapist also provided training in progressive muscle relaxation, deep breathing, and mindfulness exercises.

Kai's first attempt to reach out to the housing office resulted in them being in tears. The person on the phone kept using their legal name and misgendering them, and eventually Kai ended the call because they felt overwhelmed. They could not speak due to their anxiety becoming heightened. They did not leave their dorm room for a few days and in the next therapy session, the provider worked with Kai to identify the types of automatic thoughts that were triggered by this experience and the underlying core belief that Kai was unworthy. In response to this, the provider could use a variety of techniques to support Kai in developing more helpful beliefs about their capacity and worth. Kai felt validated and heard by the provider and was open to trying again to advocate for a room change. This time, they practiced some physiological self-soothing prior to the call (e.g., deep breathing), and they asked to make the call during the session so that they could have support if needed. This time, Kai started the call by telling the person their affirmed name and pronouns. The housing office assistant was receptive and used their affirmed name throughout, with just a few slipups with pronouns. Kai was able to learn the information they needed about changing dorms and submitted a request for this change to start next semester. A single dorm room would be more expensive, but Kai decided to take out a higher student loan to cover the cost as the benefits to their emotional well-being felt important. After the call, the provider discussed Kai's takeaways from the experience and noted specific self-advocacy strategies that may benefit them in the future and that "sometimes, but not always, our worst fears come true." This flexibility in thinking about situations will be important to improving Kai's anxiety in the long run. The therapist could explore creating a hierarchy and using exposure exercises to help Kai approach other situations that induce anxiety for them. The therapist should be mindful of the realistic potential for danger. The therapist could engage Kai in a dialogue about the potential for danger and harm in each of the scenarios in the hierarchy, use imaginal exposures, and create a safety plan to help address these concerns.

Another focus of therapy could be learning to externalize stigmas. Kai had a thin wall between others' perceptions of them and how they viewed themselves. For trans people, there will likely always be some external rejection that they will have to navigate and manage. When these messages are internalized, they result in heightened anxiety, depression, and suicidality for many trans people. In therapy, Kai worked on learning to differentiate their own views of themselves from what was rooted in others' transphobia. Through that process, they were able to identify a number of unique strengths associated with being genderqueer which bolstered their self-esteem. The provider could also discuss with Kai their values and the concept of values-based living. Through increasing their engagement in experiences that Kai found personally meaningful, Kai's feelings of being unworthy and hopeless may diminish.

Later in therapy, Kai expressed readiness to start hormones and at that stage, the provider wrote a letter of support, which was sent to their medical provider after acquiring the appropriate release of information. In this case, there was little additional assessment needed as the information needed for a letter had already been obtained over the 8 months that Kai had been in therapy. Again, it is important to keep in mind that Kai was seeking therapy at intake. Therapy is not a prerequisite for gender affirming medical care, and Kai was not required to go to therapy in order to receive this letter. When clients are seeking hormones, they may have an inaccurate understanding that they need therapy in order to obtain a letter. The therapist could provide psycho-education about the requirements in WPATH SOC (which do not require therapy) and provide information about informed consent models, with appropriate referrals to support the client in their gender affirmation process (see Section 2.4: Informed Consent, and Section 2.6.9: Knowledge of Local Resources).

6

Further Reading

Chang, S. C., Singh, A. A., & dickey, l. m. (2018). *A clinician's guide to gender-affirming care: Working with transgender and gender nonconforming clients*. Context Press.
In this volume, Chang and colleagues have provided a text that can be used across mental health professions. The work includes questions at the end of each chapter for the client and for the provider. These questions can help to develop the affirmative clinical approach that a provider might take.

dickey, l. m. (2021). *Case studies in clinical practice with trans and gender non-binary clients: A handbook for working with children, adolescents, and adults*. Jessica Kingsley.
This work by dickey explores clinical examples across the lifespan. He develops each of the cases in a way that brings out the challenges that trans and nonbinary people often face in life. Each chapter ends with comments from an expert(s) in the field, who change to offer their own professional opinion about the case described in that chapter.

Kauth, M. R., & Shipherd, J. C. (Eds.). (2018). *Adult transgender care: An interdisciplinary approach for training mental health professionals*. Routledge.
Kauth and Shipherd have edited a text that brings together the voices of multidisciplinary providers who cover a wide range of topics. This book is especially useful for readers who are beginning to work with trans people, as it will help the reader understand the collaborative nature of affirmative practice with trans clients.

Keo-Meier, C., & Ehrensaft, D. (Eds.). (2018). *The gender affirmative model: An interdisciplinary approach to supporting transgender and gender expansive children*. American Psychological Association. https://doi.org/10.1037/0000095-000
Keo-Meier (a.k.a. St. Amand) and Ehrensaft have created a model for work with trans and gender expansive children. The experts who wrote the chapters bring their specialized knowledge to the application of the model.

Olson, J., Forbes, C., & Belzer, M. (2011). Management of the transgender adolescent. *Archives of Pediatrics & Adolescent Medicine, 165*(2), 171–176. https://doi.org/10.1001/archpediatrics.2010.275

Olson, J., Schrager, S. M., Belzer, M., Simons, L. K., & Clark, L. F. (2015). Baseline physiologic and psychosocial characteristics of transgender youth seeking care for gender dysphoria. *Journal of Adolescent Health, 57*(4), 374–380. https://doi.org/10.1016/j.jadohealth.2015.04.027
Olson has published numerous resources for working with adolescent trans clients. She is a powerful speaker as well.

Singh, A. A., & dickey, l. m. (Eds.). (2017). *Affirmative counseling and psychological practice with transgender and gender nonconforming clients*. American Psychological Association. https://doi.org/10.1037/14957-000
After the APA *Guidelines for Psychological Practice with Transgender and Gender Non-Conforming People* (APA, 2015) were published, the task force chairs realized that in the process of writing the guidelines, some topics were not fully developed. Each of the chapters covers topics with a special emphasis on work with trans people with intersecting identities and the ways in which psychologists can advocate for their clients.

7

References

American Psychiatric Association. (2013). *Diagnostic and statistical manual of mental disorders* (5th ed.).
American Psychological Association. (2008). *Transgender, gender identity, and gender expression non-discrimination.* https://www.apa.org/about/policy/transgender.pdf
American Psychological Association. (2015). Guidelines for psychological practice with transgender and gender nonconforming people. *American Psychologist, 70*(9), 832–864. https://doi.org/10.1037/a0039906
American Psychological Association. (2021). *APA resolution on gender identity change efforts.* https://www.apa.org/about/policy/resolution-gender-identity-change-efforts.pdf
Anzani, A., Morris, E. R., & Galupo, M. P. (2019). From absence of microaggressions to seeing authentic gender: Transgender clients' experiences with microaffirmations in therapy. *Journal of LGBT Issues in Counseling, 13*(4), 258–275. https://doi.org/10.1080/15538605.2019.1662359
Ashley, F. (2019). Gatekeeping hormone replacement therapy for transgender patients is dehumanising. *Journal of Medical Ethics, 45,* 480–482. https://doi.org/10.1136/medethics-2018-105293
Ashley, F. (2021). The misuse of gender dysphoria: Toward greater conceptual clarity in transgender health. *Perspectives on Psychological Science, 16*(6), 1159–1164. https://doi.org/10.1177/1745691619872987
Austin, A., Craig, S. L., & Alessi, E. J. (2016). Affirmative cognitive behavioral therapy with transgender and gender nonconforming adults. *Psychiatric Clinics of North America, 40,* 141–156. https://doi.org/10.1016/j.psc.2016.10.003
Baldwin, A., Dodge, B., Schick, V. R., Light, B., Schnarrs, P. W., Herbenick, D., & Fortenberry, J. D. (2018). Transgender and genderqueer individuals' experiences with health care providers: What's working, what's not, and where do we go from here? *Journal of Health Care for the Poor and Underserved, 29*(4), 1300–1318. https://doi.org/10.1353/hpu.2018.0097
Bazrafshan, M-R., Eidi, A., Soufi, O., & Delam, H. (2021). Common psychological and behavioral disorders in transgender people: An epidemiological review. *Journal of Health Sciences & Surveillance System, 9*(1), 13–19. https://doi.org/10.30476/jhsss.2020.87675.1120
Beck, A. T. (1993). *Beck Hopelessness Scale (BHS).* Pearson.
Beck, A. T., Steer, R. A., & Brown, G. K. (1996). *Beck Depression Inventory-II (BDI-II).* Pearson.
Beckman, K., Shipherd, J., Simpson, T., & Lehavot, K. (2018). Military sexual assault in transgender veterans: Results from a nationwide survey. *Journal of Traumatic Stressors, 31*(2), 181–190. https://doi.org/10.1002/jts.22280
Benjamin, H. (1966). *The transsexual phenomenon: All the facts about the changing of sex through hormones and surgery.* Warner Books.
Berger, J. C., Green, R., Laub, D. R., Reynolds, C. L., Jr., Walker, P. A., & Wollman, L. (1979). *Standards of care: The hormonal and surgical sex reassignment of gender dysphoric persons.* Janus Information Facility.
Berke, D. S., & Sloan, C. A. (2019, November 21–24). *How to apply cognitive behavioral principles to transgender care: An evidence-based transdiagnostic framework* [Conference session]. Association for Behavioral and Cognitive Therapies convention,

Atlanta, GA. https://www.eventscribe.com/2019/ABCT/searchGlobal.asp?mode=speakers&SearchQuery=berke

Borgogna, N. C., McDermott, R. C., Aita, S. L., & Kridel, M. M. (2018). Anxiety and depression across gender and sexual minorities: Implications for transgender, gender nonconforming, pansexual, demisexual, asexual, queer, and questioning individuals. *Psychology of Sexual Orientation and Gender Diversity, 6*(1), 54–63. https://doi.org/10.1037/sgd0000306

Bränström, R., & Pachankis, J. E. (2020). Reduction in mental health treatment utilization among transgender individuals after gender-affirming surgeries: A total population study. *American Journal of Psychiatry, 177*(8), 727–734. https://doi.org/10.1176/appi.ajp.2019.19010080

Brewster, E. M., Velez, B. L., Deblaere, C., & Moradi, B. (2011). Transgender individuals' workplace experiences: The applicability of sexual minority measures and models. *Journal of Counseling Psychology, 59*(1), 60–70. https://doi.org/10.1037/a0025206

Brooks, V. R. (1981). *Minority stress and lesbian women*. Lexington Books, D. C. Health.

Bruessow, D. M., O'Connor, L. M., Eaman, E., & Chamikles, J. N. (2019). Transgender patients: Considerations for the family physician. *Family Doctor: A Journal of the New York State Academy of Family Physicians, 7*(3), 36–41. https://static1.squarespace.com/static/55771948e4b05b32926e99d0/t/5c4ccc2bc74c50461d24a88a/1548536878527/Family-Doctor-Winter2019-WEB.pdf#page=36

Brugha, T. S., McManus, S., Bankhart, J., Scott, F., Purdon, S., Smith, J., Bebbington, P., Jenkins, R., & Meltzer, H. (2011). Epidemiology of autism spectrum disorders in adults in the community in England. *Archives of General Psychiatry, 68*(5), 459–465. https://doi.org/10.1001/archgenpsychiatry.2011.38

Budge, S. L. (2015). Psychotherapists as gatekeepers: An evidence-based case study highlighting the role and process of letter writing for transgender clients. *Psychotherapy, 52*(3), 287–297. https://doi.org/10.1037/pst0000034

Budge, S. L., & dickey, l. m. (2016). Barriers, challenges, and decision-making in the letter writing process for gender transition. *Psychiatric Clinics of North America, 40*(1), 65–78. https://doi.org/10.1016/j.psc.2016.10.001

Budge, S. L., & Moradi, B. (2018). Attending to gender in psychotherapy: Understanding and incorporating systems of power. *Journal of Clinical Psychology, 74*, 2014–2027. https://doi.org/10.1002/jclp.22686

Budge, S. L., Rossman, H. K., & Howard, K. A. S. (2014). Coping and psychological distress among genderqueer individuals: The moderating effect of social support. *Journal of LGBT Issues in Counseling, 8*, 95–17. https://doi.org/10.1080/15538605.2014.853641

Budge, S. L., Sinnard, M. T., & Hoyt, W. T. (2021). Longitudinal effects of psychotherapy with transgender and nonbinary clients: A randomized controlled pilot trail. *Psychotherapy, 58*(1), 1–11. https://doi.org/10.1037/pst0000310

Butcher, J. N., Graham, J. R., Ben-Porath, Y. S., Tellegen, A., Dahlstrom, W. G., & Kaemmer, B. (2001). *MMPI-2 (Minnesota Multiphasic Personality Inventory-2): Manual for administration, scoring, and interpretation* (rev. ed.). University of Minnesota Press.

Calati, R., Ferrari, C., Brittner, M., Oasi, O., Olié, E., Carvalho, A. F., & Courtet, P. (2019). Suicidal thoughts and behaviors and social isolation: A narrative review of the literature. *Journal of Affective Disorders, 245*, 653–667. https://doi.org/10.1016/j.jad.2018.11.022

Catelan, R. F., Costa, A. B., & Lisboa, C. S. M. (2017). Psychological interventions for transgender persons: A scoping review. *International Journal of Sexual Health, 29*(4), 325–337. https://doi.org/10.1080/19317611.2017.1360432

Chang, S. C., Singh, A. A., & dickey, l. m. (2018). *A clinician's guide to gender-affirming care: Working with transgender and gender nonconforming clients*. Context Press.

Chew, D., Anderson, J., Williams, K., May, T., & Pang, K. (2018). Hormonal treatment in young people with gender dysphoria: A systemic review. *Pediatrics, 141*(4), e20173742. https://doi.org/10.1542/peds.2017-3742

Clarke, D. M., & Kissane, D. W. (2002). Demoralization: Its phenomenology and importance. *Australian and New Zealand Journal of Psychiatry, 36*, 733–742. https://doi.org/10.1046/j.1440-1614.2002.01086.x

Clarke, T. C., Schiller, J. S., & Boersma, P. (2020). *Early release of selected estimates based on data from the 2019 National Health Interview Survey.* https://www.cdc.gov/nchs/data/nhis/earlyrelease/EarlyRelease202009-508.pdf

Crenshaw, K. (1991). Mapping the margins: Intersectionality, identity politics, and violence against women of color. *Stanford Law Review, 43*(6), 1241–1299. https://doi.org/10.2307/1229039

Deogracias, J. J., Johnson, L. L., Meyer-Bahlburg, H. F. L., Kessler, S. J., Schober, J. M., & Zucker, K. J. (2007). The Gender Identity/Gender Dysphoria Questionnaire for Adolescents and Adults. *Journal of Sex Research, 44*(4), 370–379. https://doi.org/10.1080/00224490701586730

De Pedro, K. T., Gilreath, T. D., Jackson, C., & Esqueda, M. C. (2017). Substance use among transgender students in California public middle and high schools. *Journal of School Health, 87*(7), 303–309. https://doi.org/10.1111/josh.12499

de Vries, A. L. C., Kreukels, B. P. C., Steensma, T. D., Doreleijers, T. A. H., & Choen-Kettenis, P. T. (2011). Comparing adult and adolescent transsexuals: An MMPI-2 and MMPI-A study. *Psychiatry Research, 186,* 414–418. https://doi.org/10.1016/j.psyres.2010.07.033

Dhejne, C., Öberg, K., Arver, S., & Landén, M. (2014). An analysis of all applications for sex reassignment surgery in Sweden, 1960–2010: Prevalence, incidence, and regrets. *Archives of Sexual Behavior, 43,* 1535–1545. https://doi.org/10.1007/s10508-014-0300-8

dickey, l. m. (2016). Transgender inclusion in the LGBTQ rights movement. In A. E. Goldberg (Ed.), *The SAGE encyclopedia of LBGTQ studies* (pp. 1224–1226). Sage.

dickey, l. m. (2020). History of gender identity and mental health. In E. Rothblum (Ed.), *The Oxford handbook of sexual and gender minority mental health* (pp. 25–32). Oxford University Press.

dickey, l. m., & Budge, S. L. (2020). Suicide and the transgender experience: A public health crisis. *American Psychologist, 75*(3), 380–390. https://doi.org/10.1037/amp0000619

dickey, l. m., Burnes, T. R., & Singh, A. A. (2012). Sexual identity development of female-to-male transgender individuals: A Grounded Theory inquiry. *Journal of LGBT Issues in Counseling, 6*(2), 118–138. https://doi.org/10.1080/15538605.2012.678184

dickey, l. m., Reisner, S. L., & Juntunen, C. L. (2015). Non-suicidal self-injury in a large online sample of transgender adults. *Professional Psychology: Research and Practice, 46*(1), 3–11. https://doi.org/10.1037/a0038803

DuBois, L. Z., Puckett, J. A., & Langer, S. J. (2021). Development of the Gender Embodiment scale: Trans masculine spectrum. *Transgender Health.* Advance online publication. http://doi.org/10.1089/trgh.2020.0088

Ekins, R., & King, D. (2005). Virginia Prince: Pioneer of transgendering. *International Journal of Transgenderism, 8,* 5–15. https://doi.org/10.1300/J485v08n04_02

Felitti, V. J., Anda, R. F., Nordenberg, D., Williamson, D. F., Spitz, A. M., Edwards, V., Koss, M. P., & Marks, J. S. (1998). Relationship of childhood abuse and household dysfunction to many of the leading causes of death in adults: The Adverse Childhood Experiences (ACE) study. *American Journal of Preventive Medicine, 14*(4), 245–258. https://doi.org/10.1016/s0749-3797(98)00017-8

Fisher, C. M., Irwin, J. A., & Coleman, J. D. (2014). LGBT health in the midlands: A rural/urban comparison of basic health indicators. *Journal of Homosexuality, 61,* 1062–1090. https://doi.org/10.1080/00918369.2014.872487

Flentje, A., Heck, N. C., & Sorenson, J. L. (2014). Characteristics of transgender individuals entering substance abuse treatment. *Addictive Behaviors, 39*(5), 969–975. https://doi.org/10.1013/j.addbeh.2014.01.011

Flores, A. R., Herman, J. L., Gates, G. J., & Brown, T. N. T. (2016). *How many adults identify as transgender in the United States?* https://williamsinstitute.law.ucla.edu/wp-content/uploads/Trans-Adults-US-Aug-2016.pdf

Fox Tree-McGrath, C. A., Puckett, J. A., Reisner, S. L., & Pantalone, D. W. (2018). Sexuality and gender affirmation in transgender men who have sex with cisgender men. *International Journal of Transgenderism, 19,* 389–400. https://doi.org/10.1080/15532739.2018.1463584

Freire, P. (1970). *Pedagogy of the oppressed.* Continuum.

Galupo, M. P., & Pulice-Farrow, L. (2020). Subjective ratings of gender dysphoria scales by transgender individuals. *Archives of Sexual Behavior, 49*(2), 479–488. https://doi.org/10.1007/s10508-019-01556-2

Harrison, J., Grant, J., & Herman, J. L. (2012). A gender not listed here: Genderqueers, gender rebels, and otherwise in the National Transgender Discrimination Study. *LGBTQ Public Policy Journal at the Harvard Kennedy School, 2*(1), 13–24. https://escholarship.org/uc/item/2zj46213

Hays, P. A. (2016). *Addressing cultural complexities in practice: Assessment, diagnosis, and therapy* (3rd ed.). American Psychological Association.

Hendricks, M. L., & Testa, R. J. (2012). A conceptual framework for clinical work with transgender and gender nonconforming clients: An adaptation of the minority stress model. *Professional Psychology: Research and Practice, 43,* 460–467. https://doi.org/10.1037/a0029597

Hollinsaid, N. L., Weisz, J. L., Chorpita, B. F., Skov, H. E., the Research Network on Youth Mental Health, & Price, M. A. (2020). The effectiveness and acceptability of empirically supported treatments in gender minority youth across four randomized controlled trials. *Journal of Consulting and Clinical Psychology, 88*(12), 1053–1064. https://doi.org/10.1037/ccp0000597

Holt, N. R., Hope, D. A., Mocarski, R., & Woodruff, N. (2018). First impressions online: The inclusion of transgender and gender nonconforming identities and services in mental healthcare providers' online materials in the USA. *International Journal of Transgenderism, 20,* 49–62. https://doi.org/10.1080/15532739.2018.1428842

Holt, N. R., Huit, T. Z., Shulman, G. P., Meza, J. L., Smyth, J. D., Woodruff, N., Mocarski, R., Puckett, J. A., & Hope, D. A. (2019). Trans Collaborations Clinical Check-In (TC^3): Initial validation of a progress monitoring measure for transgender and gender non-conforming adults receiving psychological services. *Behavior Therapy, 50,* 1136–1149. https://doi.org/10.1016/j.beth.2019.04.001

Horvath, K. J., Iantaffi, A., Swinburne-Romine, R., & Bockting, W. (2014). A comparison of mental health, substance use, and sexual risk behaviors between rural and non-rural transgender persons. *Journal of Homosexuality, 61,* 1117–1130. https://doi.org/10.1080/00918369.2014.872502

Huebner, D. M., Thoma, B. C., & Neilands, T. B. (2015). School victimization and substance use among lesbian, gay, bisexual, and transgender adolescents. *Prevention Science, 16*(5), 734–743. https://doi.org/10.1007/s11121-014-0507-x

Human Rights Campaign. (n.d.). *San Francisco transgender benefit: Estimating cost and utilization for the "worst case" (1997–2001).* https://www.thehrcfoundation.org/professional-resources/san-francisco-transgender-benefit-estimating-cost-and-utilization-for-the-worst-case-1997-2001

Irwin, J. A., Coleman, J. D., Fisher, C. M., Marasco, V. M. (2014). Correlates of suicide ideation among LGBT Nebraskans. *Journal of Homosexuality, 61,* 1172–1191. https://doi.org/10.1080/00918369.2014.872521

James, S. E., Herman, J. L., Rankin, S., Keisling, M., Mottet, L., & Anafi, M. (2016). *The report of the 2015 U.S. Transgender Survey.* National Center for Transgender Equality. https://transequality.org/sites/default/files/docs/usts/USTS-Full-Report-Dec17.pdf

Jones, B. A., Bouman, W. P., Haycraft, E., & Arcelus, J. (2019). The Gender Congruence and Life Satisfaction Scale (GCLS): Development and validation of a scale to measure outcomes from transgender health services. *International Journal of Transgenderism. 20*(1), 63–80. https://doi.org/10.1080/15532739.2018.1453425

Kashubeck-West, S., Whieley, A. M., Vossenkemper, T., Robinson, C., & Deitz, C. (2017). Conflicting identities: Sexual minority, transgender, and gender nonconforming individuals navigating between religion and gender-sexual orientation identity. In K. A. DeBord, A. R. Fischer, K. J. Bieschke, & R. M. Perez (Eds.). *Handbook of sexual orientation and gender diversity in counseling and psychotherapy* (pp. 213–238). American Psychological Association. https://doi.org/10.1037/05959-009

Kattari, S. K., Curley, K. M., Bakko, M., & Misiolek, B. A. (2020). Development and validation of the Trans-Inclusive Provider Scale. *American Journal of Preventive Medicine, 58,* 707–714. https://doi.org/10.1016/j.amepre.2019.12.005

Kauth, M. R., & Shipherd, J. C. (Eds.). (2018). *Adult transgender care: An interdisciplinary approach for training mental health professionals.* Routledge.

Keo-Meier, C. L., & Fitzgerald, K. M. (2017). Affirmative psychological testing and neurocognitive assessment with transgender adults. *Psychiatric Clinics of North America, 40*(1), 51–64. https://doi.org/10.1016/j.psc.2016.10.011

Keo-Meier, C. L., Herman, L. I., Reisner, S. L., Pardo, S. T., Sharp, C., & Babcock, J. C. (2015). Testosterone treatment and MMPI-2 improvement in transgender men: A prospective controlled study. *Journal of Consulting and Clinical Psychology, 83*(1), 143–156. https://doi.org/10.1037/a0037599

King, W. M., & Gamarel, K. E. (2020). A scoping review examining social and legal gender affirmation and health among transgender populations. *Transgender Health, 6*(1), advance online publication. http://doi.org/10.1089/trgh.2020.0025

Klemmer, C. L., Arayasirikul, S., & Raymond, H. F. (2018). Transphobia-based violence, depression, and anxiety in transgender women: The role of body satisfaction. *Journal of Interpersonal Violence, 36*(5-6), 2633–2655. https://doi.org/10.1177/0886260518760015

Kosciw, J. G., Clark, C. M., Truong, N. L., & Zongrone, A. D. (2020). *The 2019 National School Climate Survey.* GLSEN. https://www.glsen.org/research/2019-national-school-climate-survey

Kosciw, J. G., Greytak, E. A., & Diaz, E. M. (2009). Who, what, where, when, and why: Demographic and ecological factors contributing to hostile school climate for lesbian, gay, bisexual, and transgender youth. *Journal of Youth and Adolescence, 38,* 976–988. https://doi.org/10.1007/s10464-009-9412-1

Kosciw, J. G., Palmer, N. A., & Kull, R. M. (2015). Reflecting resiliency: Openness about sexual orientation and/or gender identity and its relationship to well-being and educational outcomes for LGBT students. *American Journal of Community Psychology, 55,* 167–178. https://doi.org/10.1007/s10964-009-9412-6

Krug, G. E., Dahlberg, L. L., Mercy, A. J., Zwi, A., & Lozano, R. (Eds.). (2002). *World report on violence and health.* World Health Organization.

Kroenke, K., Spitzer, R. L., & Williams, J. B. W. (2001). The PHQ-9: Validity of a brief depression severity measure. *Journal of General Internal Medicine, 16*(9), 606–613. https://doi.org/10.1046/j.1525-1497.2001.016009606.x

Lefevor, G. T., Sprague, B. M., Boyd-Rogers, C. C., & Smack, A. C. P. (2019). How well do various types of support buffer psychological distress among transgender and gender nonconforming students? *International Journal of Transgenderism, 20*(1), 39–48. https://doi.org/10.1080/15532739.2018.1452172

Leibowitz, S. (2021). *Foundations in gender development in children and adolescents* [Webinar]. World Professional Association for Transgender Health. https://www.wpath.org/gei

Levine, S. B., Brown, G. R., Coleman, E., Cohen-Kettenis, P. T., Van Maasdam, J., Pfäfflin, F. & Schafer, L. (1998). *Standards of care for gender identity disorders* (5th ed.). Harry Benjamin Gender Dysphoria Association.

Lindsay, J. A., Keo-Meier, C., Hudson, S., Walder, A., Martin, L. A., & Kauth, M. R. (2016). Mental health of transgender veterans of the Iraq and Afghanistan conflicts who experiences military sexual trauma. *Journal of Traumatic Stress, 29*(6), 563–567. https://doi.org/10.1002/jts.22146

Littman, L. L. (2018). Parent reports of adolescents and young adults perceived to show signs of a rapid onset of gender dysphoria. *PLoS ONE, 13,* Article 0202330. https://doi.org/10.1371/journal.pone.0202330

Lovibond, S.H., & Lovibond, P.F. (1995). *Manual for the Depression Anxiety Stress Scales* (2nd ed.). Psychology Foundation.

Matsuno, E. (2019). Nonbinary-affirming psychological interventions. *Cognitive and Behavioral Practice, 26*(4), 617–628. https://doi.org/10.1016/j.cbpra.2018.09.003

Matsuno, E., & Israel, T. (2018). Psychological interventions promoting resilience among transgender individuals: Transgender Resilience Intervention Model (TRIM). *The Counseling Psychologist, 46*(5), 632–655. https://doi.org/10.1177/0011000018787261

McIntosh, P. (1989). White privilege: Unpacking the invisible knapsack. *Peace and Freedom*. https://psychology.umbc.edu/files/2016/10/White-Privilege_McIntosh-1989.pdf

Meyer, I. H. (2003). Prejudice, social stress, and mental health in lesbian, gay, and bisexual populations: Conceptual issues and research evidence. *Psychological Bulletin, 129*, 674–697. https://doi.org/10.1037/0033-2909.129.5.674

Millet, N., Longworth, J., & Arcelus, J. (2016). Prevalence of anxiety symptoms and disorders in the transgender population: A systemic review of the literature. *International Journal of Transgenderism, 18*(1), 27–38. https://doi.org/10.1080/15532739.2016.1258353

Morris, E. R., Lindley, L., & Galupo, M. P. (2020). "Better issues to focus on": Transgender microaggressions as ethical violations in therapy. *The Counseling Psychologist, 48*(6), 883–915. https://doi.org/10.1177/0011000020924931

Movement Advancement Project (MAP). (2021). *Snapshot: LGBTQ equality by state*. https://www.lgbtmap.org/equality-maps

Murad, M. H., Elamin, M. B., Zumaeta Garcia, M., Mullan, R. J., Murad, A., Erwin, P. J., & Montori, V. M. (2010). Hormonal therapy and sex reassignment: A systematic review and meta-analysis of quality of life and psychosocial outcomes. *Clinical Endocrinology, 72*, 214–231. https://doi.org//10.1111/j.1365-2265.2009.03625.x

Nadal, K. L. (2013). *That's so gay! Microaggressions and the lesbian, gay, bisexual, and transgender community*. American Psychological Association.

The National Child Traumatic Stress Network. (2021). *Complex trauma*. https://www.nctsn.org/what-is-child-trauma/trauma-types/complex-trauma

Nobili, A., Glazebrook, C., Bouman, W. P., Glidden, D., Baron-Cohen, S., Allison, C., Smith, P., & Arcelus, J. (2018). Autistic traits in treatment-seeking transgender adults. *Journal of Autism and Developmental Disorders, 48*, 3984–3994. https://doi.org/10.1007/s10803-018-3557-2

Nuttbrock, L., Bockting, W., Rosenblum, A., Hwahng, S., Mason, M., Macri, M., & Becker, J. (2014). Gender abuse, depressive symptoms, and substance abuse among transgender women: A 3-year prospective study. *American Journal of Public Health, 104*, 2199–2206. https://doi.org/10.2105/AJPH.2014.302106

Olson, K. R., Durwood, L., DeMeules, & McLaughlin, K. A. (2016). Mental health of transgender children who are supported in their identities. *Pediatrics, 137*(3), 1–8 (e20153223). https://doi.org/10.1542/peds.2015-3223

Pachankis, J. E. (2018). The scientific pursuit of sexual and gender minority health treatments: Toward evidence-based affirmative practice. *American Psychologist, 73*(9), 1207–1219. https://doi.org/10.1037/amp0000357

Pachankis, J. E., & Safren, S. A. (2019). *Handbook of evidence-based mental health practice with sexual and gender minorities*. Oxford University Press. https://doi.org/10.1093/med-psych/9780190669300.001.0001

Peitzmeier, S. M., Hughto, J. M. W., Potter, J., Deutsch, M. B., & Reisner, S. L. (2019). Development of a novel tool to assess intimate partner violence against transgender individuals. *Journal of Interpersonal Violence, 34*(11), 2376–2397. https://doi.org/10.1177/0886260519827660

Puckett, J. A. (2019). An ecological approach to therapy with gender minorities: Special issue commentary. *Cognitive and Behavioral Practice, 26*, 254–269. https://doi.org/10.1016/j.cbpra.2019.08.002

Puckett, J. A., Cleary, P., Rossman, K., Mustanski, B., & Newcomb, M. (2018). Barriers to gender-affirming care for transgender and gender nonconforming individuals. *Sexuality Research and Social Policy, 15*, 48–59. https://doi.org/10.1007/s13178-017-0295-8

Radix, A., Sevelius, J., & Deutsch, M. B. (2016). Transgender women, hormonal therapy and HIV treatment: A comprehensive review of the literature and recommendations for best practices. *Journal of the International AIDS Society, 19*(352), 1–8. https://doi.org/10.7448/IAS.19.3.20810

Reisner, S. L., White Hughto, J. M., Gamarel, K. E., Keuroghlian, A. S., Mizock, L., & Pachankis, J. (2016). Discriminatory experiences associated with posttraumatic stress disorder symptoms among transgender adults. *Journal of Counseling Psychology, 63*(5), 509–519. https://doi.org/10.1037/cou0000143

Restar, A. J. (2020). Methodological critique of Littman's (2018) parental-respondents accounts of "rapid onset gender dysphoria." *Archives of Sexual Behavior, 49,* 61–66. https://doi.org/10.1007/s10508-019-1453-2

Richmond, K. A., Burnes, T., & Carroll, K. (2012). Lost in trans-lation: Interpreting systens of trauma for transgender clients. *Traumatology, 18*(1), 45–57. https://doi.org/10.1177/1534765610396726

Rood, B. A., Maroney, M. R., Berman, A. K., Puckett, J. A., Reisner, S. L., & Pantalone, D. W. (2017). Identity concealment in transgender adults: A qualitative examination of minority stress and gender affirmation. *American Journal of Orthopsychiatry, 87,* 704–713. https://doi.org/10.1037/ort0000303

Rosenkrantz, D. E., Black, W. W., Abreu, R. L., Aleshire, M. E., & Fallin-Bennett, K. (2017). Health and health care of rural sexual and gender minorities: A systematic review. *Stigma and Health, 2,* 229–243. https://doi.org/10.1037/sah0000055

Ryan, C. Heubner, D., Diaz, R. M., & Sanchez, J. (2009). Family rejection is a predictor of negative health outcomes in white and Latino lesbian, gay, and bisexual young adults. *Pediatrics, 123*(1), 346–352. https://doi.org/10.1542/peds.2007-3524

Schulz, S. L. (2018). The informed consent model of transgender care: An alternative to the diagnosis of gender dysphoria. *Journal of Humanistic Psychology, 58*(1), 72–92. https://doi.org/10.1177/0022167817745217

Sheldrick, R. C., Benneyan, J. C., Giserman Kiss, I., Briggs-Gowan, M. J., Copeland, W., & Carter, A. S. (2015). Thresholds and accuracy in screening tools for early detection of psychopathology. *Journal of Child Psychology and Psychiatry, 56*(9), 936–948. https://doi.org/10.1111/jcpp.12442

Shipherd, J. C., Maguen, S., Skidmore, W. C., & Abramovitz. (2011). Potentially traumatic events in a transgender sample: Frequency and associated symptoms. *Traumatology, 17*(2), 56–67. https://doi.org/10.1177/1553476561039561

Shulman, G. P., Holt, N. R., Hope, D. A., Mocarski, R., Eyer, J., & Woodruff, N. (2017). A review of contemporary assessment tools for use with transgender and gender nonconforming adults. *Psychology of Sexual Orientation and Gender Diversity, 4*(3), 304–313. https://doi.org/10.1037/sgd0000233

shuster, s. m. (2019). Performing informed consent in transgender medicine. *Social Science & Medicine, 226,* 190–197. https://doi.org/10.1016/j.socscimed.2019.02.053

Singh, A. A. (2016). Moving from affirmation to liberation in psychological practice with transgender and gender nonconforming clients. *American Psychologist, 71*(8), 755–762. https://doi.org/10.1037/amp0000106

Singh, A. A., & dickey, l. m. (2017). Introduction. In A. A. Singh & l. m. dickey (Eds.), *Affirmative counseling and psychological practice with transgender and gender nonconforming clients* (pp. 3–18). American Psychological Association.

Singh, A. A., Hays, D. G., & Watson, L. S. (2011). Strength in the face of adversity: Resilience strategies of transgender individuals. *Journal of Counseling & Development, 89*(1), 20–27. https://doi.org/10.1002/j.1556-6678.2011.tb00057.x

Singh, A., Meng, S. E., & Hansen, A. W. (2014). "I am my own gender": Resilience strategies of trans youth. *Journal of Counseling and Development, 92,* 208–218. https://doi.org/10.1002/j.1556-6676.2014.00150.x

Sloan, C. A., & Berke, D. S. (2018). Dialectical behavior therapy as a treatment option for complex cases of gender dysphoria. In M. R. Kauth & J. C. Shipherd (Eds.), *Adult transgender care: An interdisciplinary approach for training mental health professionals.* (pp. 123–139). Routledge. https://doi.org/10.4324/9781315390505-8

Sloan, C. A., & Shipherd, J. C. (2019). An ethical imperative: Effectively reducing SGM disparities utilizing a multi-level intervention approach. *Cognitive and Behavioral Practice, 26*(2), 239–242. https://doi.org/10.1016/j.cbpra.2019.02.001

Smith, B. W., Dalen, J., Wiggins, K., Tooley, E., Christopher, P., & Bernard, J. (2008). The Brief Resiliency Scale: Assessing the ability to bounce back. *International Journal of Behavioral Medicine, 15,* 194–200. https://doi.org/10.1080/10705500802222972

Society of Counseling Psychology. (2020). *The resource for incorporating trans and gender diverse issues into counseling psychology curricula.* https://socpd1.memberclicks.net/

index.php?option=com_content&view=article&id=460:connect---resource-trans-and-gender-diverse-issues&catid=20:site-content

Spitzer, R. L., Kroenke, K., Williams, J. B. W., & Löwe, B. (2006). A brief measure for assessing generalized anxiety disorder. *Archives of Internal Medicine, 166,* 1092–1097. https://doi.org/10.1001/archinte.166.10.1092

Steensma, T. D., McGuire, J. K., Kreukels, B. P. C., Beekman, A. J., & Cohen-Kettenis, P. T. (2013). Factors associated with desistence and persistence of childhood gender dysphoria: A quantitative follow-up study. *Journal of the American Academy of Child & Adolescent Psychiatry, 52*(6), 582–590. https://doi.org/10.1016/j.jaac.2013.03.016

Steinle, K. (2011). Hormonal management of the female-to-male transgender patient. *Journal of Midwifery & Women's Health, 56,* 293–302. https://doi.org/10.1111/j.1542-2011.2011.00037.x

Substance Abuse Mental Health Services Administration. (2015). *Ending conversion therapy: Supporting and affirming LGBTQ youth.* https://store.samhsa.gov/product/Ending-Conversion-Therapy-Supporting-and-Affirming-LGBTQ-Youth/SMA15-4928

Tebbe, E. A., & Moradi, B. (2016). Suicide risk in transgender populations: An application of Minority Stress Theory. *Journal of Counseling Psychology, 63*(5), 520–533. https://doi.org/10.1031/cou0000152

Testa, R. J., Habarth, J., Peta, J., Balsam, K., & Bockting, W. (2015). Development of the Gender Minority Stress and Resilience Measure. *Psychology of Sexual Orientation and Gender Diversity, 2*(1), 65–77. https://doi.org/10.1037/sgd0000081

Testa, R. J., Michaels, M. S., Bliss, W., Rogers, M. L., Balsam, B. F., & Joiner, T. (2017). Suicidal ideation in transgender people: Gender minority stress and interpersonal theory factors. *Journal of Abnormal Psychology, 126*(1), 125–136. https://doi.org/10.1037/abn0000234

Thomas, R., Pega, F., Khosla, R., Verster, A., Hana, T., & Say, L. (2017). Ensuring an inclusive global health agenda for transgender people. *Bulletin of the World Health Organization, 95,* 154–156. https://doi.org/10.2471/BLT.16.183913

Thorne, N., Witcomb, G. L., Neider, T., Nixon, E., Yip, A., & Arcelus, J. (2019). A comparison of mental health symptomatology and levels of social support in young treatment seeking transgender individuals who identify as binary and non-binary. *International Journal of Transgenderism, 20*(2–3), 241–250. https://doi.org/10.1080/15532739.2018.1452660

Thrower, E., Bretherton, I., Pang, K. C., Zajac, J. D., & Cheung, A. S. (2020). Prevalence of autism spectrum disorder and attention-deficit hyperactivity disorder amongst individuals with gender dysphoria: A systematic review. *Journal of Autism and Developmental Disorders, 50,* 695–706. https://doi.org/10.1007/s10803-019-04298-1

Turban, J. L. (2018). Potentially reversible social deficits among transgender youth. *Journal of Autism and Developmental Disorders, 48,* 4007–4009. https://doi.org/10.1007/a10803-018-3603-0

Turban, J. L., King, D., Reisner, S. L., & Keuroghlian, A. S. (2019). Psychological attempts to change a person's gender identity from transgender to cisgender: Estimated prevalence across the US states: 2015. *American Journal of Public Health, 109*(10), 1452–1454. https://doi.org/10.2105/ajph.2019.305237

US Department of Health and Human Services. (2021). *Section 1557 of the Patient Protection and Affordable Care Act.* https://www.hhs.gov/civil-rights/for-individuals/section-1557/index.html

Villarroel, M. A., & Terlizzi, E. P. (2020). *Symptoms of depression among adults: United States, 2019* (NCHS Data Brief, no. 379). US Department of Health and Human Services, Centers for Disease Control and Prevention. https://www.cdc.gov/nchs/data/databriefs/db379-H.pdf

Walinsky, D., & Whitcomb, D. (2010). Using the ACA Competencies for Counseling with Transgender Clients to increase rural transgender well-being. *Journal of LGBT Issues in Counseling, 4*(3–4), 160–175. https://doi.org/10.1080/15538605.2010.524840

Warrier, V., Greenberg, D. M., Weir, E., Buckingham, C., Smith, P., Lai, M-C., Allison, C., & Baron-Cohen, S. (2020). Elevated rates of autism, other neurodevelopmental and psychiatric diagnoses, and autistic traits in transgender and gender-diverse individuals. *Nature Communications, 11,* 3959–3971. https://doi.org/10.1083/s41467-020-17794-1

Wernick, J. A., Busa, S., Matouk, K., Nicholson, J., & Janssen, A. (2019). A systemic review of the psychological benefits of gender-affirming surgery. *Urologic Clinics of North America, 46,* 475–486. https://doi.org/10.1016/j.ucl.2019.07.002

Whitehead, J., Shaver, J., & Stephenson, R. (2016). Outness, stigma, and primary health care utilization among rural LGBT populations. *PLoS ONE, 11,* Article e0146139. https://doi.org/10.1371/journal.pone.0146139

White Hughto, J. M., & Reisner, S. L. (2016). A systemic review of the effects of hormone therapy on psychological functioning and quality of life in transgender individuals. *Transgender Health, 1*(1), 21–31. https://doi.org/10.1089/trgh.2015.0008

Wiepjes, C. M., Nota, N. M., de Blok, C. J. M., Klaver, M., de Vries, A. L. C., Wensing-Kruger, S. A., de Jongh, R. T., Bouman, M-B., Steensma, T. D., Cohen-Kettenis, P., Gooren, L. J. G., Kreukels, B. P. C., & den Heijer, M. (2018). The Amsterdam cohort of gender dysphoria study (1972–2015): Trends in prevalence, treatment, and regrets. *Journal of Sexual Medicine, 15,* 582–590. https://doi.org/10.1016/j.jsxm.2018.01.016

Woodrum, T. D., Mizock, L., Vivian, J., Ormerod, A. J., & dickey, l. m. (2021). Demoralization among TGD individuals: Distinctness from depression and associations with community connectedness and wellbeing. *Stigma & Health.* Advance online publication.

World Health Organization. (n.d.). *WHO/Europe brief-transgender health in the context of ICD*-11. https://www.euro.who.int/en/health-topics/health-determinants/gender/gender-definitions/whoeurope-brief-transgender-health-in-the-context-of-icd-11

World Professional Association for Transgender Health. (2012). *Standards of care for the health of transsexual, transgender, and gender nonconforming people* (7th version). https://www.wpath.org/publications/soc

Appendix: Tools and Resources

The materials reproduced on the following pages can also be downloaded free of charge from the Hogrefe website after registration.

Appendix 1: Client Case Conceptualization Form
Appendix 2: Sources for Finding Providers
Appendix 3: Training Resources
Appendix 4: Client Reading
Appendix 5: List of Biographical Resources
Appendix 6: Sample Letters
Appendix 7: List of Established Conferences

How to proceed:

1. Create a user account (or, if you have already one, please log in)

For customers from the USA, Canada, and the rest of the world:
hgf.io/login-us

For European customers:
hgf.io/login-eu

2. Download your supplementary materials

Go to **My supplementary materials** in your account dashboard and enter the code below. You will automatically be redirected to the download area, where you can access and download the supplementary materials.

Code: B-89SK9F

To make sure you have permanent direct access to all the materials, we recommend that you download them and save them on your computer.

Client Case Conceptualization Form

Client characteristics and presenting problem:

Distal stressors:

(e.g., discrimination, rejection, victimization, harassment, misgendering, nonaffirmation)

Proximal stressors:

(e.g., internalized stigma, expectations or rejection, identity concealment)

Social narratives and lived environment:

(e.g., narratives about trans people's lives, futures, and identities; gendered environments and contexts; legal landscape; political context)

Relational context:

(e.g., familial and interpersonal relationships, resources)

Adapted from *How to Apply Cognitive Behavioral Principles to Transgender Care: An Evidence-Based Transdiagnostic Framework* [Conference session], by D. S. Berke and C. A. Sloan. Association for Behavioral and Cognitive Therapies Convention, Atlanta, GA, November 21–24, 2019.

This page may be reproduced by the purchaser for personal/clinical use.
From: l. m. dickey and J. A. Puckett: *Affirmative Counseling for Transgender and Gender Diverse Clients*

© 2023 Hogrefe Publishing

Sources for Finding Providers

Finding a provider who works with trans and gender nonconforming people is sometimes challenging. We offer the following online resources but make no guarantee as to the results of a search, meaning that there could be providers who are not affirmative in their work with trans people also listed on such websites. Providers should seek more detailed information about any referrals before taking their expertise and knowledge at face value.

Resource	Web address
Psychology Today	https://www.psychologytoday.com/us
American Psychological Association	https://locator.apa.org/
World Professional Association for Transgender Health (WPATH)	https://wpath.org/provider/search/
Gay Lesbian Medical Association (GLMA)	https://glmaimpak.networkats.com/
OutCare	https://www.outcarehealth.org/
Gender Affirming Letter Access Project	https://thegalap.org/
Association for Behavioral and Cognitive Therapies	https://www.findcbt.org/FAT/

Training Resources

Many mental health providers seek opportunities to gain additional training in work with transgender and gender nonbinary people. Some of the conferences listed in Appendix 7 "List of Established Conferences" hold a parallel conference that is intended to focus on the needs of providers. Providers in this case may include mental or physical health professionals. The following organizations are known to have programs that are designed to provide training on ways to work with trans people. The authors of this book make no guarantee of the content that any of these programs offer.

- **The Gender U**. This program currently offers *The Gender Affirmative Supportive Surgery Evaluation Tool* (ASSET). This tool can be used to assess a client's readiness for surgery. https://thegenderu.com/

- **LGBT Health Policy & Practice Program**. This program is offered through George Washington University in Washington, DC. This distance-learning program is designed as a graduate certificate that focuses on health issues and the reduction of health disparities. https://lgbt.columbian.gwu.edu/

- **National LGBTQIA+ Health Education Center**. As a part of the Fenway Institute, this program offers numerous online resources for addressing the needs of LGBTQIA+ people. Topics for the training offerings include behavioral health, hormone therapy, addressing the health care needs of trans people living with HIV, legal issues, and work with trans youth. https://www.lgbtqiahealtheducation.org/

- **PESI**. PESI is a nonprofit organization that offers inperson and online training on a wide variety of topics including work with trans clients. The list of course options can be found on their website (https://www.pesi.com/).

- **Transgender Training Institute**. This organization is led by people with trans and nonbinary identities. They offer a wide variety of training topics for individuals and organizations. Additionally, they provide supervision and a train-the-trainer course that provides the requisite training to allow participants to gain knowledge and efficacy in addressing topics related to trans people and their needs. https://www.transgendertraininginstitute.com/

- **World Professional Association for Transgender Health** (WPATH). WPATH has designed multiday training programs as part of their Global Education Initiative. This program trains people in the best practices in medical and mental health care. There are two tracks to certification. One assumes that a person will complete the necessary coursework offered by WPATH. The other allows people with 10 or more years of experience to document their training and knowledge and therefore not need to take the basic courses. There is also an advanced track. Advanced training can be hard to find. https://www.wpath.org/

Client Reading

There are numerous memoir-type books that may be useful. The books listed here are primarily focused on the needs of trans people and their families.

Brill, S., & Kennedy, L. (2016). *The transgender teen: A handbook for parents and professionals supporting transgender and non-binary teens.* Cleis Press.

Brill, S., & Pepper, R. (2008). *The transgender child: A handbook for families and professionals.* Cleis Press.

Erickson-Schroth, L. (Ed.). (2014*). Trans bodies, trans selves: A resource for the transgender community.* Oxford University Press. [Note: A new edition of this book will be published in 2022.]

Gromko, L. (2015). *Where's my book? A guide for transgender and gender non-conforming youth, their parents, and everyone else.* Bainbridge Books.

Singh, A. A. (2018). *The queer and transgender resilience workbook: Skills for navigating sexual orientation and gender expression.* New Harbinger.

Testa, R. J., Coolhart, D., & Peta, J. (2015). *The gender quest workbook: A guide for teens & young adults exploring gender identity.* Instant Help Books.

List of Biographical Resources

There are many memoirs of trans people's lives. This is a short list that includes nonbinary lives, Black, Indigenous, and people of color (BIPOC) stories, trans men, trans women, parents, cross dressers, adults, and youths. These are listed in alphabetical order by the title of the book. There are many more; this is not a full list.

- *About a Girl: A Mother's Powerful Story of Raising Her Transgender Child* by Rebekah Robertson
- *Always Anastacia: A Transgender Life in South Africa* by Anastacia Tomson
- *Annie's Plaid Shirt* by Stacy B. Davids & Rachel Balsaitis
- *Audacity: Memoirs of Transitioning* by Mr. M Greg Green
- *The Autobiography of a Transgender Scientist* by Ben Barres
- *Becoming a Man: The Story of a Transition* by P. Carl
- *Becoming Eve: My Journey From Ultra-Orthodox Rabbi to Transgender Woman* by Abby Stein
- *Becoming Nicole* by Nicole Maines
- *Before I Had the Words: On Being a Transgender Young Adult* by Skylar Kergil & Schuyler Bailar
- *Before My Warranty Runs Out: Human, Transgender, and Environmental Rights Advocate* by Joanna (Sister Mary Elizabeth) Clark & Margot Wilson
- *Being Jazz: My Life as a (Transgender) Teen* by Jazz Jennings
- *The Bold World: A Memoir of Family and Transformation* by Jodie Patterson
- *Christine Jorgensen: A Personal Autobiography* by Christine Jorgensen
- *Conundrum* by Jan Morris
- *Crossing: A Memoir* by Deidre N. McCloskey
- *Dear Senthuran* by Akwaeke Emezi
- *Do You Know Who I Once Was? A Story of an Unlikely Journey to Become One's True Self* by Cami Richardson
- *Embrace Your Truth: A Journey of Authenticity* by Gabrielle Claiborne & Linda Tatro Herzer
- *Fierce Femmes and Notorious Liars: A Dangerous Trans Girl's Confabulous Memoir* by Kai Cheng Thom
- *Finding Purpose: One Transgender Woman's Journey* by Patricia Elane Trimble
- *Found in Transition: A Mother's Evolution During Her Child's Gender Change* by Paria Hassouri
- *From Both Sides Now: One Woman's Journey to Love and Living Life to its Fullest* by Alexus Sheppard
- *God Doesn't Make Mistakes: Confessions of a Transgender Christian* by Laura Suzanne Scott
- *Good Boy: My Life in Seven Dogs* by Jennifer Finney Boylan
- *The GSA Club* by L. Strait-Bodey
- *Hiding From Myself: My Complicated Rebirth Into Womanhood and My Own Skin* by Amber Rose Washington
- *How We do Family: From Adoption to Trans Pregnancy, What We Learned About Love and LGBTQ Parenthood* by Trystan Reese
- *I Have Always Been Me: A Memoir* by Precious Brady-Davis & Joey Soloway
- *I Promised Not to Tell: Raising a Transgender Child* by Cheryl B. Evans
- *I'm Afraid of Men* by Vivek Shraya
- *I've Always Wanted a Daughter: A Memoir of Parenting a Transgender Child* by Ofrit Matzas
- *It Never Goes Away: Gender Transition at a Mature Age* by Anne Lauren Koch

- *The Last Time I Wore a Dress* by Daphne Scholinski & Jane Meredith Adams
- *Leaving Isn't the Hardest Thing: Essays* by Lauren Hough
- *Life Without Pockets: My Long Journey Into Womanhood* by Carla Anne Ernst
- *Love Lives Here: A Story of Thriving in a Transgender Family* by Amanda Jette Knox
- *Man Alive: A True Story of Violence, Forgiveness, and Becoming a Man* by Thomas Page McBee
- *Mommy Issues: A Mini Memoir* by Jansen Dominik Niccals
- *My Life in Transition: A Super Late Bloomer Collection* by Julia Kaye
- *My Sister: How One Sibling's Transition Changed Us Both* by Selena Leyva & Marizol Leyva
- *The Natural Mother of the Child: A Memoir of Nonbinary Parenthood* by Krys Malclm Belc
- *Not Just a Tomboy: A Trans Masculine Memoir* by Caspar J. Baldwin
- *Once a Girl, Always a Boy: A Family Memoir of a Transgender Journey* by Jo Ivester
- *Paper Genders: Pulling the Mask Off the Transgender Phenomenon* by Walt Heyer
- *A Queer and Pleasant Danger: A Memoir* by Kate Bornstein
- *Raising Ryland: Our Story of Parenting a Transgender Child With No Strings Attached* by Hillary Whittington
- *Raising Them: Our Adventures in Gender Creative Parenting* by Kyl Myers & Joey Soloway
- *Redefining Realness: My Path to Womanhood, Identity, Love, & So Much More* by Janet Mock
- *The Secrets of My Life* by Caitlyn Jenner
- *Self-Made Man: An Autobiography of a Black Transgender Man* by Kevin Thompson
- *She Said She Said: Love, Loss, & Living My New Normal* by Anne M Reid
- *She's Not There: A Life in Two Genders* by Jennifer Finney Boylan
- *Sissy: A Coming-of-Gender Story* by Jacob Tobia
- *Skirting Gender: Life and Lessons of a Crossdresser* by Vera Wylde & Sarah Brown
- *Some Assembly Required: The Not-So-Secret Life of a Transgender Teen* by Arin Andrews
- *Sometimes It Hurts: A Transgender Woman's Journey* by Allison Whitaker
- *Spellbound: A Graphic Memoir* by Bishakh
- *Stuck in the Middle: A Memoir of Parenting in Three Genders* by Jennifer Finney Boylan
- *The Trauma Cleaner: One Woman's Extraordinary Life in Death, Decay, and Disaster* by Sarah Krasnostein
- *Tomorrow Will Be Different: Love, Loss, and the Fight for Trans Equality* by Sarah McBride
- *Top to Bottom: A Memoir and Personal Guide Through Phalloplasty* by Finlay Games
- *Trans Like Me: Conversations for All of Us* by C. N. Lester
- *Trans: A Memoir* by Juliet Jaques & Sheila Heti
- *Two Spirits, One Heart: A Mother, Her Transgender Son, and Their Love and Acceptance* by Marsha Alzumi & Aiden Alzumi
- *Uncomfortable Labels: My Life as a Gay Autistic Trans Woman* by Laura Kate Dale
- *What We Will Become: A Mother, a Son, and a Journey of Transformation* by Mimi Lemay
- *Where's the Mother? Stories From a Transgender Dad* by Trevor MacDonald
- *Without Shame: Learning to Be Me* by Connelly Akstens
- *A Year Without a Name: A Memoir* by Cyrus Dinham
- *Yes, You are Trans Enough: My Transition From Self-Loathing to Self-Love* by Mia Violet

Sample Letters

Following is a sampling of the types of letters that a psychologist may need to write on behalf of their clients. Depending on the purpose of the letter, it may be important to understand the guidelines that the letter recipient is following. The most prominent set of guidelines for letter writing can be found in the World Professional Association for Transgender Health (WPATH) Standards of Care (2012). In Section 4.3: Variations of the Method: Letter Writing, we have provided a list of the generally required elements based on the Standards of Care. Below we provide samples of letters commonly requested by clients. For the sake of simplicity, we use nonbinary pronouns.

Referral for Hormone Treatment

I am writing today to refer Alex Howard to you for hormone treatment. Alex (DOB: 1/1/2000) has been working with me for 6 months. Alex is of the age of majority, has engaged in an informed consent process, and has a long history of identifying as trans.

I am a licensed, board-certified counseling psychologist. I have written and spoken extensively about working with transgender and gender nonbinary people in the mental health setting. Although I consider myself a generalist in working with clients, my specialty is working with trans people.

Alex began seeing me as they had questions about their gender. Alex meets the criteria for gender dysphoria. They were also concerned about experiences of anxiety and occasional panic attacks. As we worked through their gender questions and as Alex learned some coping skills, their experiences of anxiety have largely remitted.

Given Alex's identity, it is appropriate to initiate hormone treatment at this time. Alex has a good understanding of the risks and benefits of hormone treatment and also knows what to expect regarding changes in their body. We will continue to work together to ensure that Alex has the support they need. The initiation of hormone treatment is medically necessary for Alex.

Alex is a senior in college and lives with three roommates. These roommates are supportive and also have LGBTQ+ identities. Alex came out to their parents earlier this year and received a tepid response. Given their academic progress and the fact that they are scheduled to start a professional job, they are well-positioned to move forward in their life.

Should there be any questions about Alex or our work together, I can be reached by phone at (222) 555-1234 or by email at no@no.com. Thank you in advance for your care with Alex.

Referral for Chest Surgery

I am writing today to refer Alex Howard to you for chest surgery. Alex (DOB: 1/1/2000) has been working with me for 6 months. Alex is of the age of majority, has engaged in an informed consent process, and has a long history of identifying as trans. Alex meets the criteria for gender dysphoria.

I am a licensed, board-certified counseling psychologist. I have written and spoken extensively about working with transgender and gender nonbinary people in the mental health setting. Although I consider myself a generalist in working with clients, my specialty is working with trans people.

Alex began seeing me after having been on hormones for 6 months. Alex's hormones are managed by Dr. Jeffrey's at the Main Clinic. Given Alex's identity, it is appropriate to schedule surgery at this time. Alex has a good understanding of the risks and benefits of surgery and also knows what to expect regarding changes in their body. Chest surgery is a medically necessary treatment for Alex. We will continue to work together to ensure that Alex has the support they need.

Alex is a senior in college and lives with three roommates. These roommates are supportive and also have LGBTQ+ identities. Alex will have the support of these roommates after surgery, and one of the roommates who has completed this surgery has a good knowledge of how to best support Alex.

Should there be any questions about Alex or our work together, I can be reached by phone at (222) 555-1234 or by email at no@no.com. Thank you in advance for your care with Alex.

Referral for Genital Surgery

I am writing today to refer Alex Howard to you for genital surgery. Alex (DOB: 1/1/2000) has been working with me for 6 months. Alex is of the age of majority, has engaged in an informed consent process, and has a long history of identifying as trans. Alex meets the criteria for gender dysphoria.

I am a licensed, board-certified counseling psychologist. I have written and spoken extensively about working with transgender and gender nonbinary people in the mental health setting. Although I consider myself a generalist in working with clients, my specialty is working with trans people.

Alex began seeing me as they feel ready to have genital surgery. They were also concerned about symptoms of depression. As we have worked together, Alex has gained some coping skills, and their symptoms of depression have largely remitted. It is important to note that Alex does not have a history of suicidal ideation or behavior. Alex sees Dr. Velo at the Main Clinic for medication management. Dr. Velo has also written a letter in support of Alex's desire to complete genital surgery.

Given Alex's identity and the length of time on hormones (for 13 months), it is appropriate to complete genital surgery at this time. Alex has a good understanding of the risks and benefits of surgery. We have talked at great length about the challenges that may lay ahead and types of complications to attend to should they arise. Genital surgery is a medically necessary treatment for Alex. We will continue to work together to ensure that Alex has the support they need.

Alex has a stable job. They have had this job for 5 years. They are reportedly well-respected in their workplace. Alex lives alone. They have already made arrangements to secure support from a nursing service that will look in on them after surgery, as needed. This is the same nursing service that is recommended by your office.

Should there be any questions about Alex or our work together, I can be reached by phone at (222) 555-1234 or by email at no@no.com. Thank you in advance for your care with Alex.

Referral Regarding Identity Documents

I am writing today on behalf of Alex (given name Alexandria) Howard. Alex was born on 1/1/2000. I have Alex's permission to write this letter to you.

Alex was assigned {sex assigned at birth}. Alex has been under my treatment for gender dysphoria. They have been on hormones for over a year and present as {insert appropriate gender here} in all aspects of their life. It is important that Alex have identity documents that are consistent with their expressed gender.

Should there be any questions about this request, I can be reached by phone at (222) 555-1234 or by email at no@no.com. Thank you in advance for your care with Alex.

Classroom Accommodations

Note. Although this is a letter that you can write, you may choose to work with an administrative office at the student's school. You can use this text as a template for the letter.

I am writing on behalf of Alexandria Howard (ID #123456). This student is enrolled in PSY 123 Section 12 for the Fall of 2022. Alex uses the pronouns they/them/their and goes by the name Alex. It is my sincere hope that you will honor this request by using the correct name and pronouns with Alex.

Should there be any questions about this request, I can be reached by phone at (222) 555-1234 or by email at no@no.com. Thank you in advance for your care with Alex.

Carry Letter

Note. Trans people sometimes need a letter that can be provided to officials and other people in positions of authority (e.g., police). This letter, which should make sense as you read it, can be used to help address situations in which a trans person is providing identification that is not consistent with their gender expression.

I am writing on behalf of Alexandria Howard (DOB: 1/1/2000). Alexandria goes by the name Alex, and they have a nonbinary gender identity, although they were assigned female at birth.

Alex has asked me to write this letter as they realize that the way they express their gender may not be consistent with your expected perception based on the gender marker on their identification. Although Alex may not appear to be dressed in a manner you might be expecting, I hope that you will treat them with dignity and respect.

Should there be any questions about this request, I can be reached by phone at (222) 555-1234 or by email at no@no.com. Thank you in advance for your care with Alex.

List of Established Conferences

This is not an exhaustive list. Additionally, conditions such as the pandemic have affected many conference opportunities. You are encouraged to conduct your own research about these and other conference opportunities.

Advancing Excellence in Transgender Health (Boston, MA)
Black Trans Advocacy Conference (Dallas, TX)
Diva Las Vegas (Las Vegas, NV)
The EDGY Conference (North Hills, CA)
Esprit (Port Angeles, WA)
Fantasia Fair (Provincetown, MA)
First Event (Waltham, MA)
Five College Queer Gender & Sexuality Conference (Amherst, MA)
Gender Education De-Mystification Symposium (GEMS; Atlanta, GA)
Gender Infinity (Houston, TX)
Gender Odyssey (Seattle, WA, & San Diego, CA)
Imperial Court of Massachusetts (Boston, MA)
Imperial Court of Rhode Island (Providence, RI)
Keystone Conference (Harrisburg, PA)
National Trans Health Summit (Oakland, CA)
New York Coming Out International Transgender Conference (New York City, NY)
Out & Equal (Las Vegas, NV)
Philadelphia Trans Wellness Conference (Philadelphia, PA)
Southern Comfort Transgender Conference (Fort Lauderdale, FL)
Sparkle (Manchester, UK)
TransCon (Miami, FL)
TRANSforming Gender Conference (Boulder, CO)
Transgender Lives Conference (Hartford, CT)
Trans Leadership Summit (Northridge, CA)
TransOhio Trans & Ally Symposium (Burton, OH)
True Colors Annual Conference (Hartford, CT)
Virginia Transgender Information & Empowerment Summit (Richmond, VA)
WPATH Biennial Symposium (location varies)

Advances in Psychotherapy
Evidence-Based Practice

All volumes of the series at a glance

- **Alcohol Use Disorders** (Vol. 10)
- **Alzheimer's Disease and Dementia** (Vol. 38)
- **ADHD in Adults** (Vol. 35)
- **ADHD in Children and Adolescents** (Vol. 33)
- **Autism Spectrum Disorder** (Vol. 29)
- **Binge Drinking and Alcohol Misuse Among College Students and Young Adults** (Vol. 32)
- **Bipolar Disorder** (Vol. 1, 2nd ed.)
- **Body Dysmorphic Disorder** (Vol. 44)
- **Childhood Maltreatment** (Vol. 4, 2nd ed.)
- **Childhood Obesity** (Vol. 39)
- **Chronic Illness in Children and Adolescents** (Vol. 9)
- **Chronic Pain** (Vol. 11)
- **Depression** (Vol. 18)
- **Eating Disorders** (Vol. 13)
- **Elimination Disorders in Children and Adolescents** (Vol. 16)
- **Generalized Anxiety Disorder** (Vol. 24)
- **Growing Up with Domestic Violence** (Vol. 23)
- **Headache** (Vol. 30)
- **Heart Disease** (Vol. 2)
- **Hoarding Disorder** (Vol. 40)
- **Hypochondriasis and Health Anxiety** (Vol. 19)
- **Insomnia** (Vol. 42)
- **Internet Addiction** (Vol. 41)
- **Language Disorders in Children and Adolescents** (Vol. 28)
- **Mindfulness** (Vol. 37)
- **Multiple Sclerosis** (Vol. 36)
- **Nicotine and Tobacco Dependence** (Vol. 21)
- **Nonsuicidal Self-Injury** (Vol. 22)
- **Obsessive-Compulsive Disorder in Adults** (Vol. 31)
- **Persistent Depressive Disorders** (Vol. 43)
- **Phobic and Anxiety Disorders in Children and Adolescents** (Vol. 27)
- **Problem and Pathological Gambling** (Vol. 8)
- **Public Health Tools for Practicing Psychologists** (Vol. 20)
- **Sexual Dysfunction in Women** (Vol. 25)
- **Sexual Dysfunction in Men** (Vol. 26)
- **Sexual Violence** (Vol. 17)
- **Social Anxiety Disorder** (Vol. 12)
- **Substance Use Problems** (Vol. 15, 2nd ed.)
- **Suicidal Behavior** (Vol. 14, 2nd ed.)
- **The Schizophrenia Spectrum** (Vol. 5, 2nd ed.)
- **Treating Victims of Mass Disaster and Terrorism** (Vol. 6)
- **Women and Drinking: Preventing Alcohol-Exposed Pregnancies** (Vol. 34)

Visit **hogrefe.com/us/apt** to get more information about the series!

Prices: US $29.80 / € 24.95 per volume. Standing order price US $24.80 / € 19.95 per volume (minimum 4 successive volumes) + postage & handling. Special rates for APA Division 12 and Division 42 members

www.hogrefe.com